Teaching Primaries Today

Teaching Primaries TODAY

by
Elizabeth B. Jones

BAKER BOOK HOUSE
Grand Rapids, Michigan

Copyright 1974 by
Beacon Hill Press of Kansas City
Reprinted 1975 by
Baker Book House
ISBN: 0-8010-5061-8

Quotations from the *Revised Standard Version of the Bible*, copyrighted 1946 and 1952.

Quotations from the *New American Standard Bible*, copyright © The Lockman Foundation, 1960, 1962, 1963, 1968, 1971.

To Marti
who shares with me
her sense of wonder

Contents

Foreword	8
Acknowledgments	9
Chapter One: Teaching in Today's World	11
Chapter Two: As the Children Come	27
Chapter Three: Exploring Purposes and Materials	47
Chapter Four: Creating a Climate for Learning	70
Chapter Five: Let's Be Creative	89
Chapter Six: More Creative Methods	105
Bibliography	128

Foreword

Guiding children to Christ is important work, and the author of this book can help us.

Elizabeth Jones is a creative Christian: mother, teacher, author. Her four children, now grown, are guiding their own children into the ways of peace. For 16 years Mrs. Jones taught children and supervised their teachers in the Primary Department of her home church. Since 1958 she has guided other teachers in leadership workshops across the United States and Canada.

She has written 16 books—10 of them for children and 6 to guide Christian teachers and parents. Mrs. Jones has prepared child-centered, Bible-based teaching materials for two evangelical publishing houses. For 15 years she has edited primary curriculum materials for the Church of the Nazarene.

In *Teaching Primaries Today* the author has distilled the best from her exciting experiences. Here is understanding of the gospel; here is insight into how children learn and grow toward Christian maturity; here is a beautiful blend of love and learning.

I commend these exciting explorations to our 12,000 primary teachers and supervisors. Some of you are experienced; others are just beginning. There is challenge in this book for both of you. I rejoice in the promise here held out to 100,000 primary boys and girls who meet each Sunday morning with you. Here is the promise of a living fellowship: a loving teacher, eager children, and our Living Lord in the midst.

—A. F. HARPER
Executive Editor, Department of Church Schools
Church of the Nazarene

Acknowledgments

Many times I have wanted to share with other teachers some of my experiences in teaching primary boys and girls. When the Holy Spirit seemed to urge also, this book began to take form.

First of all, I am grateful for the leading and help of the Holy Spirit in this undertaking.

I am indebted also:

To Dr. Albert F. Harper for his urging, and for his patience and editorial expertise;

To Dr. K. S. Rice for inspiring each of us to reach out in loving concern to those around us;

To Dr. Roy E. Swim for his insight into the spiritual needs of children and into the Word of God;

To other writers in the field of Christian education and in child development, for help in deeper understanding of children and more effective ways of teaching;

To the gifted and consecrated teachers on the local church team with whom I have worked, for some of the actual experiences given;

For other incidents shared with me by the many teachers I have met in workshops and discussion groups;

And finally, to the children whom I have taught and loved, and from whom I have learned many things.

To all of these, I say, "Thank you."

Sincerely,

Elizabeth B. Jones

Chapter 1

Teaching in Today's World

Those who are wise shall shine like the brightness of the firmament; and those who turn many to righteousness, like the stars for ever and ever.
—Dan. 12:3 (RSV)

We live in an exciting and sometimes bewildering age. The world is changing from day to day at an almost unbelievable rate. A child born in the latter half of the twentieth century will experience more change in a lifetime than occurred from the time of Moses to the beginning of this century. All of us are aware of rapid change but we can scarcely grasp its meaning.

What Is Happening Today?

Man now walks on the moon and lives in space for many days. Events happening in far-off places are bounced off satellites and viewed in our own living rooms. Unmanned spacecraft probe the mysteries of faraway planets in hopes of unlocking more secrets of our universe. New discoveries in science, medicine, and education stretch our imagination and speak of greater discoveries ahead. An article written in any one of these fields is likely to be outdated even before it can be published in a current magazine.

Important changes are also taking place in the field of education. Learning becomes an exciting adventure as pupil and teacher explore and learn together. Pupils are learning to think, examine, create, discover, experiment, and appropriate. Education is no longer viewed as primarily a process of teaching facts. More emphasis is being placed on the learner's understanding and ability to relate facts to his own experience. Teachers seek also to direct learning experiences toward inquiry and a search for meaningful truth.

Mass media are an important tool in bringing understanding and insight into the customs, needs, and problems of people around the world. It is used effectively in teaching children and adults in history, arts, and sciences.

But not all that is happening in our world is good or conducive to Christian living. The mobile society in which we live creates serious problems. Families are often uprooted and moved to new environments. This may cause a breaking away from family traditions and moral standards. These mobile families often fail to find a church home in the new community. Parents and children alike are cut off from the nurture and fellowship of the Church. Studies show that such changes take a heavy toll in family life. Ethics and values may become distorted. Problem drinking and physical and mental disorders often result. Marriages may suffer, and parents may be unable to provide a healthy home environment for their children.

The mass media are largely responsible for the materialistic and secular influences prevalent in our society. People are constantly pressured to buy things: a new car, a new home, new furnishings, or the latest gadget. Little or no emphasis is placed on moral or spiritual values.

What About Today's Children?

Children do not live in a vacuum. They live and grow today in the midst of our complex society, and are greatly influenced by what they see and hear. They are in danger of losing all sense of what is sacred, and what belongs to God. How will they know what is right and what is wrong? How will they develop a sense of values? How can they build a secure faith in a world that is torn with fear and uncertainty?

And what about children from economically or culturally deprived homes where parents cannot combat the pressures of their own personal problems? Many thousands of children know nothing about a secure family life, only unhappiness and despair. Marital chaos, quarreling, and even fighting are a way of life. On the other hand, even children from affluent homes often suffer loneliness and a feeling of being unloved because parents are busy making money or keeping up social activities.

The disadvantaged, the physically handicapped, the mentally retarded, the hungry, the unloved, and the unlovely—all are in our world today waiting for some word of hope.

What Does This Say to the Church?

The Church is being challenged as never before to meet the needs of a world in turmoil. Scientists and sociologists predict that drastic and perhaps shattering change may come in the days ahead. If the Church is to meet its challenge, it must consider the trends in our society today. It must be aware of changing life-styles and seek new ways to make the gospel effective.

First of all, the Church must accept the fact of change and be willing to adjust to it. This does not mean that we will change the great truths of our faith; it does mean that we need to change our methods and ways of communicating our faith. This is especially true in the Christian education of children. We must relate what we believe to the world in which the children live.

What do all the new methods in education say to the Church as it plans to share its faith with the children? What happens when a child comes to the church school and is exposed to the age-old methods of teacher-tell, pupil-listen? Does it convey subtly that the gospel is unimportant and irrelevant to the day in which we live? Does it say that the Church is merely a place to meet friends or to be bored for an hour or so?

Consider again the impact of mass media. Children who sit in their own living rooms and watch men walk on the moon, or see sports events in another part of the world, acquire greater understandings and wider vocabularies. We must take into consideration these understandings and insights as we plan to share our Christian faith. If we fail to do so, we may underestimate our children and plan materials and learning experiences beneath their capabilities and interest.

Let's Remember

In the great explosion of knowledge and exciting discoveries today, we need to keep pace with our children intellectually. With our knowledge of the universe expanding at a fantastic rate, we must not hedge them in with a God who is too small. In a day of confusion and perplexity, we need to know where we are going and what we believe. In a society that seems to be discarding so many absolutes, we must present a clear picture of what is right and what is wrong.

We need to interpret change and new learnings in the light of the gospel and the kingdom of God. If God is to become real to our children, they must understand through us the wonder of His love and forgiveness, and the joy that comes from a life centered in Him. We must find ways to relate our Christian faith to the world in which the children live.

The gospel must speak to them first through Christian persons they know and learn to love and trust. We must help them realize the timelessness of God's love as revealed in Jesus Christ, "the same yesterday, and to day, and for ever." Then too, as we face the needs of a battered world, children must also be helped to reach out to others in loving concern.

How Can We Do This?

How can we best communicate these truths to our children? What understandings of God and His great purposes do we ourselves need? What methods can we use to make our teaching-learning processes most effective? How can we be sure our ministry to boys and girls is relevant to their present experiences and environments?

Christian education, first of all, must be based on the Bible for the content of our teaching. But we should also make use of learnings and insights in other fields for its implementation. Studies in general education will give us help in psychology, educational philosophy, and methods of teaching.

With so many new insights into the needs and developmental processes of children, we must use those that are compatible with our Christian faith. New methods of putting these findings to work will help us in our quest for goals and give us a sense of direction. (The needs and characteristics of children are discussed in Chapter 2.)

God's Plan for Growth

Our ultimate goal is to help boys and girls to become new persons in Christ, and to learn to live according to God's will. Such a goal is not reached all at once, however. If we as Christian educators are to be successful in producing mature Christians, we must take into consideration God's orderly plan.

God's plan for growth in the physical world is seen in the seasons of the year, in seedtime and harvest. First there is the careful preparation of the soil and the planting of seed. This is followed by the growing season as tender young plants are cared for and allowed to grow in the sun and rain. After these conditions are met, we look for an abundant harvest in the fall.

Teaching boys and girls is somewhat like this process of growth in nature. We take into consideration the needs and maturities of children on their own age level. We prepare their hearts and minds for the Word of God, the good Seed. We provide an atmosphere of love, understanding, and much prayer through the growing season. Then we can look forward to a joyous harvest when the child accepts the Lord Jesus as Saviour and begins to live a Christian life. We must not be impatient or try to force the child to respond beyond his understanding. We must rely on the Holy Spirit to open his delicate sensibilities and direct a personal response of saving faith from the child.

Sharing Our Faith

What we believe, we want to share with our children: our doctrine, our experience, our church history, our values and standards, our love for God, and our sense of stewardship. We share our joy and freedom in worship and our rich heritage of Christian music.

We share our Christian faith because we believe the gospel has power to change lives. We know that God is at work in our world today, offering salvation, changing lives, giving hope and purpose to daily living. We want boys and girls to know this and to respond to God's love. We want to help them learn to live according to His will, in fellowship with Him, and to abide in the Christian hope.

We may share our faith in various ways and in many places. The three most important settings are: (1) the home; (2) the church school; (3) the church congregation.

The Home

Lifelong patterns and habits are begun in the home at a very early age. This is according to God's plan which is outlined in Deut. 6:4-9:

> *Hear, O Israel: The Lord our God is one Lord:*
> *And thou shalt love the Lord thy God with all thine heart, and with all thy soul, and with all thy might.*
> *And these words, which I command thee this day, shall be in thine heart:*
> *And thou shalt teach them diligently unto thy children, and shalt talk of them when thou sittest in thine house, and when thou walkest by the way, and when thou liest down, and when thou risest up.*

Often the church school teacher is frustrated because he seems to work alone in winning boys and girls from non-Christian homes to Christ and helping them become established Christians. Children brought into the church school for only one hour on Sunday, without the support of Christian teaching and example the rest of the week, present unusual challenge. The teacher must ask himself, "How can I win Randy's parents to the Lord? How can the church surround Randy with love and concern as he seeks to live a Christian life?"

This concern sends the teacher out to knock on doors, to love, to witness, and to try to win the parents and families of his pupils to God and the church. Dedicated teachers seek to help these parents appropriate the gospel to themselves—to realize that Christ died for them, and that He lives today to make them new persons in Him. Only as parents are won and Christian homes are established can we hope to build the kingdom of God most effectively.

The Church School

The church school setting includes Sunday school,

Junior Fellowship, missionary groups, junior church, camps, children's choirs, vacation Bible school, and day-care centers—wherever the church is involved in definite times of teaching children. We need to plan carefully and to correlate curriculum materials and procedures among all these groups. Capable workers who value one another and who plan together will make the children's work in the local church much more effective.

The Church Congregation

The third setting for sharing our faith is in the church congregation itself. Here children are brought into active fellowship in the work and worship of the church. Children pray when the adults pray; they sing, bring offerings, and listen to the sermon. They experience meaningful relationships with mature, growing Christians. As children see examples of love, compassion, and forgiveness in lives transformed by the gospel, they learn something of what God is like. As they hear prayers of petition and praise, testimonies of victory, and joyful music, they realize more fully what it means to be a Christian. As they sense the presence of the Holy Spirit when He brings renewal and times of refreshing, they want to commit their lives to Christ.

The teacher realizes that God is working through the church congregation to help him accomplish His purposes with the children. He is aware also that the Holy Spirit speaks through him—and even beyond his own capabilities—to make the gospel live for the boys and girls he teaches.

The concerned church may provide worship and learning experiences on the child's own level through expanded sessions or children's church. These situations call for the most skilled and dedicated leadership. It is also important that from time to time the children be brought into the adult worship and fellowship. The pastor should be alerted in advance of such occasions and plan to help the children feel they are a part of the congregation.

The Teacher

The Teacher's Significant Role

Someone has said that curriculum is 90 percent teacher. What the teacher is may be more important than what he teaches, because a contagious Christian faith is transmitted directly from person to person. The teacher teaches tangible truths, but he is also teaching many intangibles. He shares, first of all, what he is: his commitment to Christ, his love for God, his faith, his sense of stewardship, and his love for others. A public school supervisor who was evaluating the work of a student teacher said warmly, "What she *is* shines through every act." And Henry Brooks Adams wrote: "A teacher affects eternity; he can never tell where his influence stops."

Effective teachers do not happen overnight. They become effective through a process of development and growth. A person needs a natural desire to teach and to share; but knowledge, techniques, and methods are acquired through practice and study. Teachers, even those with much creative ability, must work hard to be successful.

The Marks of a Successful Teacher

1. *Has a vital personal relationship with God.* We can't lead children to a saving knowledge of God unless we know the way ourselves. We can't share that which we do not possess. A teacher must be a person who is seeking constantly to deepen his own spiritual understanding and relationship with God. He should be discovering new meaning and new strengths in the Word of God, and seek to apply these truths to his own experiences. Sometimes it is easier to quote a Bible verse to a friend or loved one who is going through deep trial than to apply the truth to ourselves in times of need.

How can we "grow in grace, and in the knowledge of our Lord and Saviour Jesus Christ"? Regular Bible study, worship experiences at church and elsewhere, witnessing by word and deed, reading devotional books—all help us to grow as Christians. Books on prayer may be especially helpful as we seek through experience and guidance of the Holy Spirit to learn more about the "effectual fervent prayer" that avails much.

What about growing in *knowledge?* Before a teacher

begins to teach, he needs to know the basic truths that we believe. Sometimes new Christians are asked to teach in the children's departments before they have had the opportunity to learn basic beliefs and develop a vital faith of their own. This is not fair either to the new Christian or to the children.

A new Christian, however, can become an important part of the teaching team and share some special skill, while learning basic truths along with the children. Such a new teacher would read books on methods, as well as articles and books for his own spiritual growth. Since observation is another important way to learn, he should watch skilled teachers at work, attend teachers' meetings, and leadership classes and workshops.

2. *Loves children.* The effective teacher loves children, enjoys being with them, and is interested in all that concerns the child. He looks upon his associations with the child as one of the most important avenues for communicating the love of God. He knows from experience that the child will learn more about love through a warm, personal relationship than he will ever learn through conversation, stories, materials, and methods. When a teacher's chief concern is for the children and what happens to them, he will take time to be with them as much as possible, and to learn from them. Emily Post, in her book *Children Are People,* says, "No one can approach success in teaching a child without being taught by the child many, many things."

Important also is our understanding of the children we teach. A teacher must put a proper value on children—the value that Jesus placed on them when He said, "Let the children come to Me." He was never too busy to show His love and consideration for a child. Likewise a teacher is concerned with each child as a person. He trusts children and respects their opinions and abilities. He encourages each one to make decisions and to learn to live with the choices he makes. He tries to help each child learn at his own pace.

3. *Is enthusiastic.* Enthusiasm helps a person to succeed in any undertaking. It is most important in teaching. Being enthusiastic means that a teacher thinks of his pupils during the week and plans for them. He is at Sunday school early on Sunday morning. Enthusiasm finds its way into his voice and manner. It helps him convey to the children that being a Christian is an important and joyous experience. We must share our enthusiasm with the children we teach if they are to be regular in their attendance and interested in learning—particularly when they come from indifferent homes.

"I don't know what you do here on Sunday morning," said a mother to a second grade teacher, "but whatever it is, my Richard loves it. He makes us get up on Sunday morning and get him ready to come. He feels he is missing something very important if he isn't here on time."

4. *Has a pleasing personality.* A teacher should be cheerful and greet the children with a smile—even when he doesn't feel that way. He should be patient, dependable, and have a sense of humor. A teacher needs to be able to laugh with the children and to share their good times with them.

On Valentine's Day, Joyce came to Sunday school with valentines she had made for the supervisor, her teacher, and her friends. The one for the supervisor was a beautiful red heart trimmed with lace and flowers. When the supervisor opened it, she read the message: "Jesus loves *even* you." Yes, the supervisor needs a sense of humor too!

5. *Uses good tools.* A teacher's tools include lesson materials which have been carefully prepared for primary children. The teacher should study these materials and, when necessary, adapt them to his own group. Supple-

mentary materials suggested in the curriculum will help to enrich his teaching. He needs a good Bible dictionary, a concordance, and books on methods.

Helpful books are listed from time to time in the lesson materials, and a teacher should build up a personal library in his area of teaching. He needs also books of stories, files of stories clipped from story papers and other sources, a poetry file, and a picture file. Children's books to share with them should be included also.

6. *Collects enrichment materials.* The teacher is an inveterate collector. He collects everything of interest to children: stories, poems, songs, pictures, clippings, and news items. He looks for birds' nests, seedpods, cocoons, galls, shells, and rocks. On every ride in the country, every walk around the block, or in a park, he keeps his eyes open for things to enrich his teaching. Objects from other lands, curios, old things, unusual Bibles—all become teaching tools.

"If you are going to collect all these things," said a patient husband of one primary teacher, "then I am going to build you some cabinets to hold them." And he did.

7. *Plans creatively.* The creative teacher is not satisfied with simply telling a Bible story, asking questions, and using the activity books. He keeps his children alert by using a variety of methods. He uses discussion, quizzes, research, picture study, art activities such as making murals, friezes, and rebuses. He plans dramatization and role playing often. (Methods are discussed fully in Chapters 5 and 6.)

8. *Is willing to help train others.* The successful teacher is always ready to share ideas and methods with other teachers. This is particularly true where team teaching is used. The new, inexperienced teacher can gain skill and confidence by working with experienced, sympathetic teachers. (See Chapter 4.)

9. *Has concern for other children.* The concerned teacher keeps a list of children whom he can contact and invite to Sunday school and is ever alert to add names to the list. When new families move into the community, he watches to see if there are children who may be invited. A call on the newcomers with a hot dish, or a plate of freshly baked cookies on moving day opens the door to friendship.

If the teacher has children of his own, he knows that they will attract other children like a magnet. This gives opportunity to invite them to Sunday school.

If other members of the church congregation are alerted to the prospect list, they will offer names from time to time.

The children in a class or department should also be involved in reaching others. The teacher may help them to develop concern for their friends who do not attend Sunday school by asking them for names of their unchurched friends. Children may also be involved in calling on some of those on the list.

To be of real benefit, a prospect list must be accurate. He should check with parents on birthdays, likes and dislikes of the child, and special interests. He must be careful not to offend by seeming to pry into the family's personal life. His rule is: Use tact and follow the leadership of the Holy Spirit.

As he contacts new families and new prospects, he may discover real needs for prayer and supportive fellowship. He should report these needs to his pastor or church visitor, who will share these concerns with him. He is a very important link in winning new families to Christ and the church.

10. *Has self-confidence.* A teacher's self-image is important. If he lacks self-confidence or a feeling of personal worth, he needs special help from God for the work. "I can

do all things through Christ which strengtheneth me" helps each one to feel secure and confident in his work as a teacher.

Remember This

1. "Study to shew thyself approved unto God, a workman that needeth not to be ashamed" (2 Tim. 2:15).
2. "Without me ye can do nothing" (John 15:5).

For Further Study

1. What effect does our changing world have on our teaching content and procedures?
2. Make a list of experiences a primary child may have during a given period: a day, a week, a year. Discuss how teachers may make the gospel relevant to these experiences.
3. Think of the children in your congregation. Are they being exposed to the loving concern and fellowship of mature Christians? Are they a vital part of the work and worship of the church?
4. How would you answer these questions:
   Why do I teach primary children?
   What qualifications do I need to be a successful teacher?
   What skills will help me to teach effectively?
   If I lack any of these skills, what may I do to acquire them?

Chapter 2

As the Children Come

Jesus said, *"Let the children come to me, do not hinder them."*
—Mark 10:14 (RSV)

Who Are They?

Six-year-old Susan came to Sunday school full of life and energy. She went from one interest center to another to see what the children were doing. She wanted to participate in the activities of each group. Said Susan one morning, "The trouble with me is I don't know my own strength!"

Seven-year-old Richard presented another extreme. He came with lagging steps and showed little interest in any of the activities. Perhaps he had been up late the night before. Perhaps he had had barely time to dress that morning before the bus arrived. There was not even time for a bite of breakfast. No wonder Richard said one day, "I feel like a broken-down old horse."

Are there a Susan and a Richard in your group? If you have been teaching even for a short time, you are aware of the individual differences and needs of children.

Each child is unique. As he comes into the world, he will see it as no other person has seen it. God has planned for each person to be unique; we see it in many ways. He has given each child fingerprints and footprints that are different from those of every other person. Scientists also tell us that each of us has a unique design in the hairs on his head. No other person has a hair print just like yours. (Perhaps this is what Jesus meant when He said, "Even the very hairs of your head are all numbered.")

The child comes to us as a unique person because of physical factors, relationships in the home, environment, and individual rate of development. Physical factors often influence how a child feels about himself and the way he reacts to the group on Sunday morning. Children with handicaps usually present problems and challenge to the teacher.

Many children come crippled in spirit and in emotional development because of poor relationships. There may be a drunken father or mother, or no father or mother in the home. Sometimes an overprotective mother or a harsh, unloving father hinders a child's emotional growth. An overbearing older brother or sister may cause a younger child real problems.

The environment into which a child is born has a deep influence on what he will become. Attitudes toward honesty, fair play—the whole moral tone of the home—has tremendous influence on the child.

The church school should be a place where a child's uniqueness is accepted and cherished.

Levels of Child Development

According to the Swiss psychologist Piaget, there are four levels of child development:

1. *Sensory-motor period* (birth to 2 years)

Everything a child learns at this level is by sensory-motor channels. What he feels, sees, smells, tastes, and hears, he manipulates in order to learn.

2. *Preoperational period* (2 to 7 years)

A child in this period is not able to use certain mental operations which are necessary for mature reasoning and understanding. He has difficulty understanding how an object can have more than one property. How can one live in San Francisco and in California? He would have difficulty understanding the Trinity: God the Father, God the Son, and God the Holy Spirit.

   3. *Concrete operations* (7 to 11 years)

We are most concerned with this period in primary teaching. Now the child can manipulate data mentally. He can come to logical conclusions—those based on things rather than ideas. He can define, compare, contrast, and deal with the whole. However, he operates chiefly in concrete rather than in abstract terms. Thus the child in this stage is very literal-minded and has difficulty with symbolism. As he begins to leave the world of fantasy and make-believe, he demands realism. Object lessons using symbolism have little meaning for him. Real objects, activities, and games are more effective at this stage of development than verbal methods.

Children are likely to form strange ideas as they try to understand some of the terminology of our adult hymns. This is true also of difficult Bible verses and passages.

The child in this period has trouble thinking of God as a Spirit. "How can God be everywhere at once?" he wonders. We encourage him to see God's handiwork round about him, and evidences of God's love through loving persons and through God's daily provision for our needs.

   4. *Formal operations* (begin at 11 or 12 years)

Children are now able to think in abstract terms. They are able to foresee end results.

If Piaget is correct, it is easy to see why some of the things we may try to teach young children are beyond their ability to grasp and understand.

General Characteristics

After considering the uniqueness of each child, and the theory of developmental processes, are there some general characteristics on each age level that help us understand children? Those who work with children tell us there are.

As a rule, primary children are a delight to the teacher. They are active, enthusiastic, curious, and imaginative. These are years of discovery and adventure.

Let's break it down a little further and think of the children on each age level.

The Six-Year-Old

Stevie, a six-year-old, is a picture of extremes. He is apt to be difficult at times and is less cooperative than when he was five. He may always want to be first and is aggressive in competition.

Because he is growing and developing so fast, he finds it difficult to sit still for long periods of time. Thus the wise teacher plans activities that allow for moving about. The six-year-old likes to make and do things with his hands. He may want to stand instead of sit as he works. He is full of questions and is likely to have definite ideas of his own. He feels more than he is able to express verbally and needs help from his teacher to put his thoughts into words.

Stevie responds to beauty. He is interested in poetry, music, and art. The teacher takes every opportunity to make use of these interests and responses. She tries to enrich her teaching materials with beautiful pcitures, poems, songs, and objects from the out-of-doors.

Stevie wants to know about prayer, probably because he feels his need for help so often. His teacher encourages him to pray and tell his needs to God.

The six-year-old needs opportunity to use his imagination to create pictures, poems, or even short stories. He should be given things to do that make him feel important. He should also be encouraged to finish what he begins—and helped to see the results of what he is doing.

The six-year-old presents a great challenge to the teacher.

The Seven-Year-Old

The seven-year-old is usually more settled and better behaved than at six. He is likely to be a daydreamer and to dawdle at his work. He is more aware of the difference between right and wrong, and wants to do right. He shows a thoughtful interest in God and asks many questions about Him. He demands realism and wants straightforward answers to his questions.

The seven-year-old usually has a deep attachment to his teacher. He wants to sit by her and likes to be given things to do to help.

The seven is more group-conscious than the six, and likes to work on group activities. He enjoys music, especially singing. He needs many different things to do to satisfy his curiosity and stimulate his interest.

The seven-year-old is beginning to evaluate his behavior by the standards of others. He is sensitive and anxious to please. Thus he cries easily when criticized. He is inclined to be jealous of other members of the family or class group. Because of his uncertainty, he needs constant assurance of love and trust.

The seven enjoys familiar stories and verses from the Bible. He likes Bible puzzles and games, and enjoys reading from the Bible. He needs experiences that show him how God is at work in the world. Opportunities to work with God's wonders are helpful to him.

The seven-year-old especially needs to feel the nearness of God at all times.

The Eight-Year-Old

The eight-year-old is more aggressive about making

friends and likes to work on group activities. He enjoys working on committees and is capable of making plans and carrying them out. He has good ideas and likes to make up his own mind about things. He likes work that challenges him mentally; Bible quizzes, games, questions and answers, riddles, and memory work present such a challenge. Words fascinate him and he likes to discover the meaning of new ones.

Eight-year-olds like to participate in worship with other members of the group. They will usually lead in prayer if asked to do so. They want to know more about heaven, and definitely want to go there someday.

The eights usually want to be grown-up and enjoy the companionship of adults. They are interested in science and the world about them; thus it is an age of exploration and discovery.

The eight-year-old is interested in the Bible as a Book and this gives opportunity for learning more about the Bible. Children of eight usually enjoy looking up passages and verses, and discovering the location of different books of the Bible. They need to know the main theme of the Bible and something of its structure and organization.

The eight's interest in science opens the door for teaching appreciation of God as Creator and Sustainer of the universe. The child's interest in history is a good basis for teaching about the Early Church, and how our own church came to be. Missionary stories are also of great interest to him.

The eight-year-old is ready to learn more of the meaning of life as it relates to God and His kingdom. He needs to learn more about the stewardship of time, talents, and possessions. "What does God want me to be when I grow up?" is a question of great importance to the eight-year-old. He will often say, "When I grow up I will be a doctor," or astronaut, or nurse, or teacher.

The eight-year-old's ability to make decisions tells us that some are ready to accept Christ as Saviour. The alert teacher is aware of this readiness, and gives opportunity from time to time for the child to make such a decision.

Eight-year-olds should be encouraged to begin habits of daily Bible reading and prayer. They should be helped also to relate everyday experiences to the goodness and love of God.

The Needs of Children

If we are to teach with wisdom and understanding, we must know something of the emotional needs of every child. What does he need in order to grow and develop spiritually? Why do some children grow up to be healthy, happy, successful persons while others are beset by unhappiness, and emotional instability? Heredity and physical health enter in, but we can't overlook other essential ingredients if children are to develop as God intends for them to do.

The Basic Needs of Children

• *A sense of trust.* If a child is to develop faith in God, he must first have faith in people. If a child does not trust people, it is almost impossible for him to find a secure faith in God.

The first seven years of a child's life are recognized as the most important period in his emotional development. During this period faith comes into being. The child's reaching out for security begins at birth, and his early experiences form the emotional foundation upon which faith can grow. The faith of parents is contagious. But the story of God's love is what finally ignites the true spark of Christian faith.

From the very beginning, children must have a climate of love and warmth if they are to have a sense of trust or security that nurtures faith. Scientific study has proved that love, beyond all question, is the most important experience in the life of a human being. The child receives his first concept of the world through early experiences with his mother. If his mother is loving, he will learn to love. The child to whom love is denied often fails to develop mentally, emotionally, and physically. In extreme cases, such children sometimes do not learn to talk, walk, or feed themselves.

We are told that 85 percent of all mental and emotional breakdowns in youth and adults come from fears that grow out of childhood experiences. What is more damaging to a child's faith than to lose confidence in one or both parents when the home is broken? What happens to the child from the unhappy home where there is quarreling, discord, and even fighting day after day?

Psychologists tell us that, when a child is in real trouble, if those working with him can find one person in whom he has confidence, a bridge can be built to help that child. If this person does not exist for the child, there is no way of reaching him. Sometimes the loving Sunday school teacher is just that person. Her understanding, love, dependability, and devotion to God can mean security to the fearful, troubled child who comes on Sunday morning. Such a teacher can share her faith, and lead the way to faith and trust in God.

● *A sense of value.* If children are to grow and develop strong characters, they must be helped to form their own sense of values. When children are six to eight, they are most easily affected by the values and standards of the adults around them. Ideas have emotional quality and prejudices are readily formed.

What about the things that surround boys and girls

today? What kind of values are they likely to form from the radio, TV, billboards, and printed materials that daily confront them? How are children to know what is true and what is false? With parents spending less and less time with their children to help them form true values and standards, our youth are forming their values from their own peers.

When values are lacking in the home, a greater responsibility rests upon the church and Sunday school. The teacher needs great wisdom in teaching a child what is right and what is wrong without undermining respect for his parents and home. This takes much prayer and dependence upon the guidance of the Holy Spirit. Surely in this we need to remember what Jesus said about being as "wise as serpents, and harmless as doves."

Children need help from a skilled and Spirit-filled teacher to form proper values. Carefully planned open-end stories and questions may lead to a discussion of alternatives and probable consequences of acts. As children hear different views expressed, they learn about values. They need to think about problems and make choices according to Christian standards and beliefs. When problems have been analyzed, alternatives discussed, and consequences predicted, the children may be helped to evaluate or suggest a solution. The wise teacher makes use of child-centered situations in role playing or discussion which relate to the spiritual truths being taught. (More is said about role playing and discussion in Chapter 5.)

• *A sense of belonging.* Each child needs a sense of belonging. He must feel that he is important to the group and to the teacher. A child who is lacking at this point is likely to become pensive, a daydreamer, or boastful and disagreeable to cover up his real feelings.

The child who comes late on Sunday morning will probably feel cheated and not a part of the group. The teacher should therefore plan to involve the latecomer as soon as possible in the activities in progress.

Jamie was always late. He came in after the morning session was well in progress. He did not know what had gone on before and he felt left out. Consequently he immediately began to misbehave and disrupt the group's activities. The teacher had called in the home and explained the importance of Jamie arriving on time, but the problem persisted. At last the teacher decided to stop everything when Jamie arrived and explain all that had taken place. Then Jamie was able to enter into the activities and become a real part of the group. The other children understood and were helpful. For Jamie this was the solution of his behavior problem.

Extra class activities such as a Saturday afternoon in the teacher's home, a hike in the woods or park also help the child to feel a part of the group. Any happy, satisfying experience with the group, either during the week or on Sunday morning, helps the child to develop a sense of belonging.

● *A sense of achievement.* Children must have some measure of success in what they undertake or they can never be happy. Unless a child begins to build a pattern of success, how can he be successful when he grows up? Most important, how can he become a mature Christian? Living for Christ calls for the highest and best in each of us. It takes determination and courage, and these important qualities need to be developed in childhood.

As teachers we may not be able to guide all children to successful lives, but we can help many—and we can help all to better lives than they would otherwise know. Experiences in Sunday school with loving, dedicated teachers have started many children toward a successful, happy future.

Jimmy was a quiet, pensive child in the second grade.

His Sunday school teacher, retired from public school work, was aware that Jimmy was different and had serious problems. A call in the home revealed that Jimmy was doing poorly in school. He had failed for two consecutive years and was failing again. No wonder he was discouraged and depressed. The teacher discovered the main reason for his continued failure was his inability to read well. She invited him to come to her home each day after school, so that she could help him with his schoolwork. With her encouragement and help, Jimmy was able to pass his grade that year, and each succeeding year. He grew up to be a successful businessman and a Christian father. What a different story it might have been if Jimmy had not come in contact with a concerned teacher who knew how to help him!

• *A sense of personal worth.* Self-esteem is a better indicator of a child's future happiness and success than is high intelligence. The child who is unable to build some measure of self-esteem may turn to negative behavior, or withdraw from the group. A prominent judge says he has never known a delinquent who did not have a poor self-image.

A child must first of all have the approval of important adults in his life if his sense of personal worth is to grow and develop. Things we say and do can change a child's attitude for better or for worse. Each child needs to feel wanted, appreciated, and know that he is important to God, to his teacher, and to the group.

A loving touch has great meaning for children. A strong hand to grasp, a shoulder to lean on—these are important and come through where words sometimes fail. For the very young child, the lap of a loving teacher is the best equipment a classroom can have. To the child who is fearful, lacking in a sense of personal worth, what could be more reassuring than a warm hug, or a loving pat on the shoulder?

"I have a special little hug for each of my children as they come," said a teacher. "After they are promoted to the next department, many of them still come to my room first for their special hug."

"I love my teacher because I can understand her face," said a primary child.

You may help to create an atmosphere of trust and respect as you listen and use a pupil's ideas. One child's work or behavior should never be compared with that of another. A child needs praise instead of criticism, encouragement instead of discouragement. Every success he has should be emphasized and praised.

A teacher should also challenge a child to stretch his ability at times. This helps him to know that the teacher believes in him. Under-achievers are usually those who are lacking in a sense of personal worth. There is also a significant relationship between a poor self-image and the inability to read.

A primary teacher was working in her classroom early one Sunday morning. Suddenly she became aware that someone was watching her. She looked up and saw a small boy.

"I'm Billy," said the child.

The teacher smiled warmly and said, "Good morning, Billy. I'm glad to see you."

"I'm a bad boy," said Billy, "and I can't learn anything. None of my teachers at school like me."

"I like you, Billy," said the teacher. "You don't look like a bad boy to me, and I think you can learn. I need a helper this morning. Will you be my helper?"

Six weeks later Billy came early again. This time there was a smile on his face and an air of confidence as he said, "I had to come early. I'm your best helper!"

The story in between tells of a teacher's calls in the home to learn more about Billy and to understand some of the reasons for his poor self-image. She spent time with Billy himself, and had special things for him to do each Sunday. She gave him much encouragement and provided a climate of love and trust.

The building of self-confidence and a worthy self-image does not always happen as dramatically as in Billy's case. But the warm, accepting teacher can do much to build a child's sense of personal worth.

Children with Special Needs

The Disturbed Child

In one group recently a teacher realized that three of the five children present were from broken homes. Each of them had special problems and each one needed extra attention.

To recognize the disturbed child, we look for the one who is often fearful, boastful, overactive, belligerent, or overly quiet and withdrawn.

To plan effectively to help such a child, the teacher not only sees what the pupil does, but tries to understand why he does it.

To guide the disturbed child, the teacher needs to be loving and understanding, but firm; to set clear and specific limits without anger or harshness. Sometimes such a child will at first learn to trust just one person, perhaps his teacher. Role playing to show good and acceptable behavior is helpful with some children.

The Child with Learning Disabilities

There are several types of learning disabilities. The problem most readily recognized by the Sunday school teacher is the inability to read. Sometimes parents are unaware of the child's difficulty and think he is being lazy or indifferent at school. The concerned teacher may be able to counsel with such parents and help them find the right solution to the child's problems. Many public schools are providing special testing and help for these children. Clinics and special helps are also available for parents and teachers. The Sunday school teacher needs to know where to find such helps.*

The Slow Learner

Some children learn at a slower rate than others. This may be caused by physical defects such as difficulty in hearing or poor vision. It happens sometimes in low-income families where health care and cultural environment are inadequate.

Slow learners need meaningful experiences that are geared to their rate of development. Poor work habits and poor motivation are often found in the slow-learner group. Thus methods and materials that catch and hold the attention of such children are needed.

Slow learners usually feel less confident than the average child. They need to have more praise and encouragement than others. Whenever possible, notes sent home to parents praising the child's progress are helpful.

Slow learners need to be encouraged to use all their creative powers. They need self-expression through art and music experiences. The teacher should ask thought questions and help the child to learn to express himself verbally.

Such children learn best on a one-to-one basis. Thus an assistant teacher or teacher's aide to work with them is

---

*Write *Closer Look,* Box 1492, Washington, D.C.

the most important. Team teaching is also effective if one member of the team gives special time and attention to the slow learner.

Learning More About Children

How can a teacher learn more about the children she teaches? One important way is by home visitation. A teacher should set a goal of visiting in the home of each child at least once during the year, oftener if possible. Only as she calls in the home and sees the child in the home environment can she teach with sympathy and understanding. "Now that I have met Jon's parents, I know better what to expect of Jon," a teacher may say.

A child is usually delighted when the teacher takes time to call in the home. He may be somewhat self-conscious and do little talking, but the visit gives the teacher opportunity to talk with the parents and other members of the family.

It is helpful if the teacher takes a small gift for the child and for other children in the family. Story papers, puzzles, and inexpensive books make good openings for such a visit. Some teachers prefer to telephone in advance and let the parents know they are coming. Care should be taken not to embarrass the parents, and not to stay too long. Sometimes an overburdened mother needs to talk out her problems with a sympathetic listener. A teacher may be asked to pray with an ill member of the family. The home visit should always be regarded as a rich ministry and one to which the teacher looks with pleasure.

When the teacher feels unwelcome, phone calls or letters may take the place of a personal visit. But the dedicated, Spirit-filled teacher does not give up too easily on home visitation.

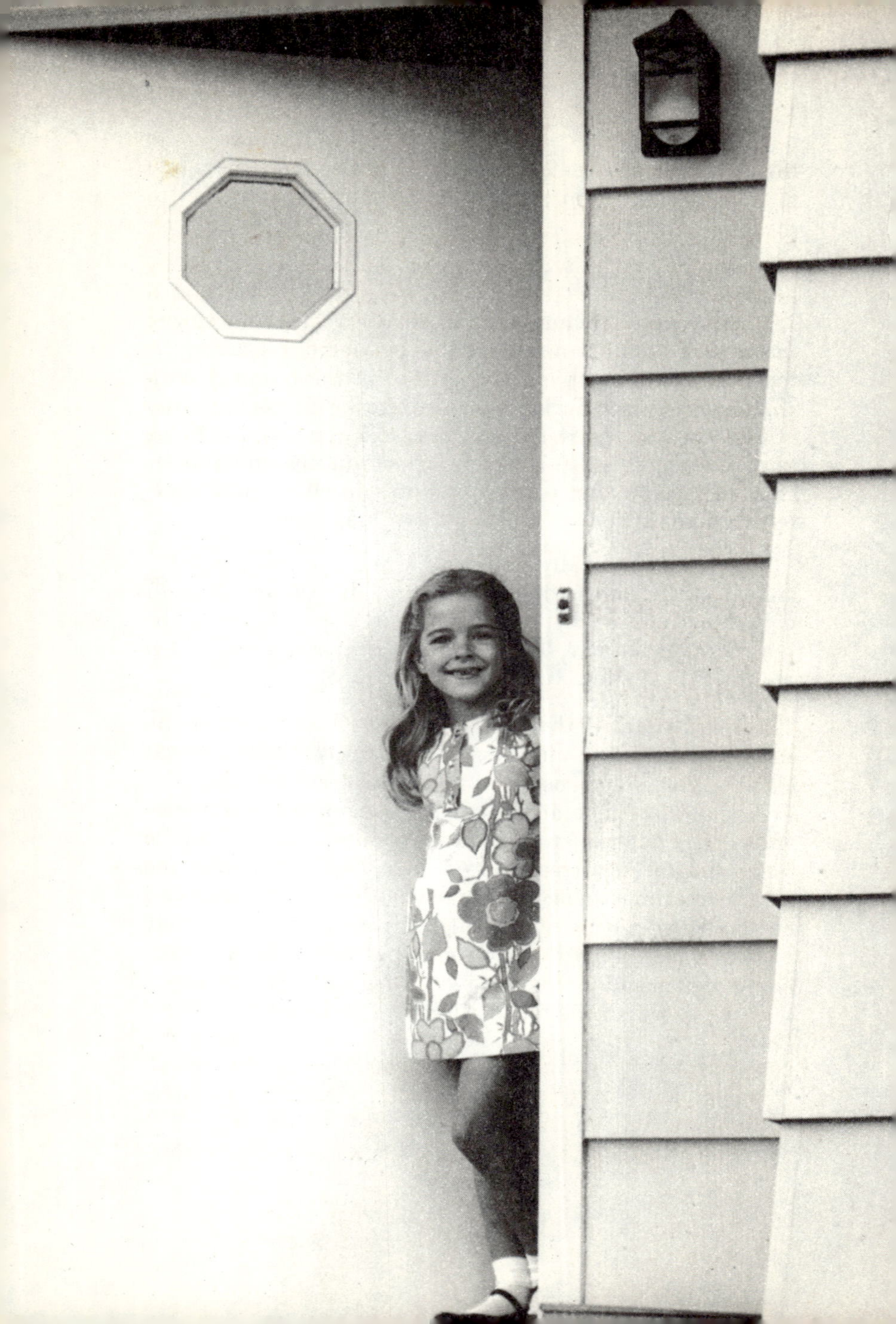

When Children Are Ill

Calls on children who are ill or shut in are most important. A small cassette recorder with a tape of the week's Bible story, songs by the children, and other interesting activities may be taken along to keep the child in touch with his class. *Primary Bible Story* booklets and story papers are useful items to take to the ill child.

Mark, a seven-year-old, was in the hospital with rheumatic fever. His Sunday school teacher, Mrs. James, made it a point each Sunday afternoon to call on Mark and share the Bible story with him. She also took along the story paper and a little gift to help Mark pass away the long hours.

One hot Sunday afternoon with the temperature around 100°, the long trip across the city seemed too much. "I don't think I will go to see Mark today," Mrs. James thought. "He probably won't miss me. He doesn't show much enthusiasm or response when I go." But this dedicated teacher could not rest with her decision. Finally she gathered up courage and went on her usual call. She visited with Mark and told him a Bible story. As she was leaving, she met Mark's mother in the hall.

"I appreciate your calls so much," the mother said, "and Mark does too. Yesterday he asked me what day of the week it was. When I said, 'Saturday,' he brightened up and said, 'Oh, good! Then tomorrow is Sunday and that is the day Mrs. James comes.'"

Mrs. James breathed a little prayer. "Thank You, Father," she said, "for the Holy Spirit's prodding today."

It is also helpful if the teacher can find opportunity to visit the child's school for open house or other times convenient for the school. The public school teacher usually welcomes such contacts, particularly with the problem child or child with learning disabilities.

The Sunday school teacher often keeps a file or notebook on each child. In this record she keeps clues about his background, family, and school life.

An interesting activity for the child which gives added information to the teacher is a family album which the child makes. Several sheets of drawing paper may be stapled together to make the album. The child may be asked to draw pictures of parents or others who care for him. Other children in the family may also be drawn. The child may draw a picture of his favorite activity or hobby. Pictures of pets or friends may be added.

The shy or withdrawn child may be encouraged to participate in a "Who Am I?" game. With the use of a tape recorder, the child describes himself, perhaps in presession away from the other children. When several children have had opportunity to record, the tape is played for the entire group and the children guess who fits the description.

Children may also be encouraged to write short biographies, "About Myself." These are exchanged in the group and children guess who is described when the biography is read aloud.

It is always a helpful and rewarding experience when teachers invite children into their homes. Sometimes two or three may be invited at a time for dinner. A teacher may take one or more out for a meal, or for a snack. Such times have deep meaning for a child and add greatly to his sense of personal worth.

What About Discipline?

An important factor in discipline is how you feel about it. Do you expect a perfectly quiet room or corner where there are no problems? Or can you accept the fact that when children are busy and happy there will be some noise? Do you expect perfection or can you be a little nearsighted and a little hard of hearing—just enough to let primary children be six and seven years of age?

The teacher needs to set limits, however, particularly for six-year-olds, and see that these limits are kept. Children are happier and learn better in a group where there is discipline based on mutual respect. The more mature seven-year-olds may be involved in helping to make rules for the group.

If you have problems, you need first of all to ask yourself some questions:

1. Am I well prepared on Sunday morning?
2. Do I have activities planned that will interest all of my pupils?
3. Am I there ahead of time, confident and relaxed, when the first child arrives?
4. Do I vary my methods from time to time, and try to involve each child?
5. Have I involved the older children in setting standards and rules of behavior? If so, are these rules simple and realistic?
6. Do I understand each pupil to the best of my ability, and realize what causes poor behavior in the problem child?
7. Have I established contact with the home and tried to build up mutual friendship and trust?
8. Do I maintain a firm but kindly manner in dealing with the children? Does my love shine through?
9. Do I avoid sarcasm? Do I try to find ways to let a child maintain his self-respect while being corrected for his behavior?
10. Have I made the problem child (or children) a special subject of prayer, asking the Holy Spirit to guide me?

When a teacher has exhausted all methods and patience, the problem child should not be allowed to disrupt the entire group. Such a child should be removed quietly and a helping teacher assigned to give him special attention. Sometimes a winsome teen-ager or a concerned older person is just the right one to help such a child. Often a child who has been isolated for a while will be able to return to the group. This is especially true where the teacher and the other children try to be supportive and redemptive in their love and fellowship.

For Further Study

1. If you have a child in your group with a poor self-image, what can you do to help him?

2. Study the activities suggested in *Primary Teacher* for the unit you are now teaching. Which of these are best suited to any slow learners that may be in your group?

3. Think of a child in your group. How would you describe his general characteristics? His uniqueness?

4. What have you observed about a pupil recently that would tell you something about the child's background? His fears? His need for assurance?

Chapter 3

Exploring Purposes and Materials

"You shall love the Lord your God with all your heart and with all your soul and with all your might."
—Deut. 6:5 (NASB)

The first and greatest commandment from the Old Testament brings into focus the truth that man is a threefold person—mind, soul, and body. The New Testament tells us that the boy Jesus grew in *wisdom* (mind), in *stature* (body), and in *favour with God and man* (spirit).

Science in its quest for knowledge has rediscovered some of the basic truths of the Word of God. This is especially true in the field of education and child development. When we plan teaching-learning experiences for children, we take into consideration the whole child—mental, spiritual, and physical. Thus we see curriculum materials planned for these three aspects of learning: knowledge, attitudes, and behavioral outcomes.

In the past, emphasis was placed on the knowledge level of learning. Thus the teacher became chiefly a dispenser of facts; he did not pay much attention to the concepts being formed or to the attitudes and feelings of the pupil. More recently, emphasis has been placed on attitudes and feelings, and on skills and other behavioral outcomes.

A report by sociologists under the direction of the National Institute of Mental Health stresses the importance of pleasure and enjoyment in the learning process.

"Pleasant, happy times in the home are essential to the child's total development," say the sociologists. This is true also in the church school. Happy, interesting experiences on Sunday morning help the child to develop mentally, spiritually, and physically. These experiences determine how a child feels about God and the church.

The Knowledge Level

The Sunday school teacher must of course be concerned with knowledge. The teaching of facts is important as we seek to transmit our Christian faith to boys and girls. We must teach them what we believe about God, Jesus, the Bible, the Church, and Christian living. Children need to learn important Bible verses and longer memory passages to use today and to store away for future use. They need to discover how our Bible came to us and how it has survived the ages. They need to learn about our church and why it came to be. They must be thoroughly familiar with the teachings of the Bible as guidelines for Christian living. They should know also something of the mission of the Church in the world today.

Attitudes and Feelings

Cognitive learning alone is not enough. The good teacher asks, "How does the child feel about what he is learning? What attitudes are being formed? What opportunities are given for the child to think, to feel, to plan, to appreciate, to carry out and evaluate? Are the methods used exciting and challenging?"

We know that how a child *feels* on Sunday morning largely determines what he learns and the concepts he forms about God and the church. Someone has said that religion is caught, not taught. Thus we realize the importance of the second level of learning: the pupil's attitudes and feelings.

Children must have a climate of love, acceptance, and

understanding in which to grow as whole persons. When a child is deprived of love in the home, it is up to the Sunday school teacher under the leadership of the Holy Spirit to fill in the gap as much as possible. Many children have been helped and encouraged to overcome a crippling home environment through loving concern from the Sunday school.

A teacher needs to ask, "How does the child feel toward me as his teacher? Am I able to communicate a feeling of warmth and love? Do I provide the atmosphere and experiences on Sunday morning that will help the the child to feel secure and to regard himself as a person of worth?"

Behavior and Skills

What about the third level of learning? Behavior development and skills mean helping boys and girls put into practice what they have learned.

How do we teach boys and girls to love God with all their strength? This involves a deep sense of stewardship through which we learn to relate all of life to God and to His kingdom. But where do we start with the child? Such a life pattern begins in the home. As parents put the teachings of Christ into practice in their daily lives, children are led to do likewise. This influence extends from the church and Sunday school also as teachers and other Christian workers speak the truth in love by example as well as words.

In an effective Sunday school, children are involved in creative activities and projects which give meaning to what they are learning. As they participate in planning and carrying out projects of helping and serving, they discover the satisfaction that comes from giving rather than receiving. As they engage in the mission of the church, they experience joy as did the disciples when they returned from doing the work of the Master (Luke 10:17).

Loving God with all the mind, soul, and body is the first and greatest commandment. It is our guideline as we involve pupils in the learning process.

Assuming Our Responsibility

When we as Christian teachers realize that children will come to know God through us, it deepens our sense of responsibility. We ask ourselves, "How can we help children to know God? What can we say and what methods can we use to bring them to know the Lord Jesus personally and to respond to Him as Saviour? How can we help them to grow in Christian ways? By what means can they be helped to relate all of life to God and His purposes?"

With a deep sense of mission, we turn to our goals and objectives.

Our curriculum materials are planned around clearly defined goals and objectives for each age-group. As a child progresses through the Sunday school from nursery through senior high, he should form concepts and values which will bring him to full maturity in Christ.

The course of study for primary children has been planned around these areas:

1. God
    a. God the Father
    b. God the Son
    c. God the Holy Spirit
2. Salvation
3. Christian Living
4. The Bible
5. The Church

1. The Primary Child and God

a. God the Father

God is Creator and Sustainer of the universe. "All things were made by him; and without him was not any thing made that was made" (John 1:3).

One of the surest ways to help children feel at home in God's world and to give them the security they so desperately need is to teach them about God, the Creator. Children are deeply interested in the world. They have a natural wonder and awe of the things they see and hear and feel. To help them serve God's handiwork in the little things about them as well as in the heavens above is to help them grow in appreciation for God, the Creator.

God not only created our world but He sustains His creation day by day. He is the Sustainer of all life; He actively maintains and controls the world that He has made. Children may be helped to see this as they observe the miracle of growing plants, new baby robins in the maple tree, and the wonder of their own growth and development, or that of a new baby in the family.

We cannot assume that the child on his own will relate these wonders to God. As parents and teachers, we need to help the child relate what he sees, hears, tastes, and touches to the wonder of God's love for him.

And most importantly, we teach children that man was created in the likeness of God, to live in fellowship with Him in this life and with Him forever in the eternal home.

God provides for life, death, growth, and change. God is the Giver of life. In His mercy He has also provided for death. Children will ask many questions concerning death and the changes it brings. Researchers tell us that the young person who is most likely to experiment with drugs, risk-taking behavior with cars, and suicide is the one whose parents have overprotected him against the finality of death. As teachers, we need to be prepared to answer children's questions about death as best we can in the light of our Christian faith.

Life also brings many changes. Loved ones move away; a home is broken; difficult circumstances bring trouble and heartache. Children should not be shielded from all these experiences. Rather they should be helped to see that, no matter what happens, God is always near with comfort and help.

God is our loving Heavenly Father. Through everyday experiences, a child may learn appreciation and gratitude for what he enjoys: food, clothing, homes, loved ones, happy times of play and work. God, our Heavenly Father, has planned homes and loving care for all. He wants us to be concerned with those who are deprived and need our help. Children who are being reared in the fellowship of the church and in Christian homes need to learn how to reach out in love to the handicapped, the disadvantaged, the lonely and sad in our world.

God is all-wise, all-powerful, and holy. Children need to know of the wisdom and power of God. As they learn to understand something of His power, it helps them to know that God is able to help at all times. Because God is holy and righteous, His love requires something of us. Children must be given an accurate picture of what is right and what is wrong. They need to know that trouble comes to those who break God's physical and moral laws. There is joy and satisfaction in doing right, but only sadness to ourselves and to others when we do wrong.

God is real and ever-present. What can we do to help children sense the reality of God? First He must be real to us if He is to become real to the children we teach. Is God real to me? Is He real to me through the experience of being a new person in Christ? Is He so real that I have consecrated my life to Him? Does His Holy Spirit abide in my heart? To be able to answer *yes* to these questions is the most effective witness we can give to the reality of God.

God also becomes real to children through Bible stories and verses, and contemporary and missionary stories. He becomes real as they experience His daily love and care and as they learn to pray and express their love and needs to Him. Through actual experiences with the world He has created—touching, tasting, seeing, smelling, and hearing—children sense the reality of God.

God is dependable. Children need to know in these troubled times that, even though everything else fails, God is always with us. When we call attention to His physical laws, we help them to know that He is dependable. The coming of day and night, the changing seasons, the tides of the sea—all speak to us of His dependable ways. The wonders of space travel and the discoveries of science are possible only because man can work with the exactness of His laws. When children understand these facts, it helps them build a firm faith and trust in God.

As mature Christians, we understand that God is sovereign in the universe. He did not create the world and then remove himself from the scene. He is actively at work in the world today and calls us to share in His great plan and purpose.

God will eventually triumph over evil. His love and power are eternal. He has promised eternal life, which begins here and prepares us for life with Him forever.

Children should be helped to feel that they too are a vital part of the great, ongoing kingdom of God. This knowledge helps children to live joyously and confidently, and calls them to commit their lives to God. It helps them to make decisions according to Christian values and principles. This truth helps them to find firm answers to their questions, "Who am I? Why am I here? Where am I going?" It also brings joy as they discover the meaning of eternal life begun here and now, and continuing forever with Jesus Christ.

God is loving and forgiving. The story of the Bible from Genesis to Revelation is the story of God's seeking, forgiving love. God reaches out to each one and invites us to come to Him. Children need to know that God always loves them, and is always ready to forgive them for their failures and wrongdoings. Boys and girls should be helped to identify God's seeking love with their own need, and to be encouraged to respond.

God reveals himself in different ways. We want primary boys and girls to discover how God has revealed himself to people. Children grow in their understanding of God's love as they learn of His self-disclosure through creation, and through the Bible and Bible people. God also reveals himself today through godly people who witness to His love—minister, parents, teachers, and others. He speaks to us through a Bible story, a verse, or quietly in our hearts as we pray and listen for Him to guide us.

God's supreme revelation is through Jesus. In Jesus God made himself and His purposes known. "He that hath seen me hath seen the Father" are the words of Jesus (John 14:9). As we help children know more about Jesus and His way of love and helpfulness, we lead them to know what God is like. Jesus came and lived among men, "to preach the gospel to the poor . . . to heal the brokenhearted, to preach . . . recovering of sight to the blind" (Luke 4:18). He came to suffer the death of the Cross for the sins of men.

b. *God the Son*

Jesus is our most important approach for teaching children about God and our Christian faith. He spoke words of wisdom to the lawyers of His day, and He cleansed the Temple with authority. But what did He do when children were brought to Him? He simply opened His arms and the children came gladly. This same Jesus has the strongest appeal for children today.

In the Christian home, children first come to know Jesus through parents and others who love and serve Him as Lord and Saviour. Jesus is the constant Companion and Helper in all of life's experiences. The first stories of Jesus shared with very young children are usually the warm, tender accounts of the Babe in the manger, the joyful news to the shepherds, and the coming of the wise men. Later, stories are told of Jesus, the loving One who went about doing good and helping people.

By the time the child reaches primary years, he is ready for a connected story of the life of Jesus. Thus the primary cycle has a study of His life beginning with the Christmas story and extending through the Crucifixion, Resurrection, and Ascension. Primary children learn how the baby Jesus grew to be a man, and began His special work. As He went about healing the sick, giving sight to the blind, preaching the gospel, and raising the dead, He was showing people what God is like. His death on the Cross for our sins was the supreme revelation of God's love. His resurrection, His ascension, and His promise to come again give hope and purpose to those who love and serve Him today.

This continued story helps primary children understand something of why Jesus came, and what His coming has meant to the whole world. They should also become aware that Jesus loves each one and invites each to respond to His love. Those who are ready may be helped to accept Him as Saviour.

Primary children should learn as much of the teachings of Jesus as are meaningful to their own experiences. "You are My friends, if you do what I command you" (John 15:14, NASB) has meaning for boys and girls as they try to follow Jesus' commandment to love one another. The golden rule to treat others as they would be treated makes a difference in what they say and do at home, at school, and on the playground.

Primaries should share in Christian concerns for the world. As they learn about Christ's command to go into all the world with the good news of the gospel, they should have a part in sharing the good news. They need to be related to the total mission of the Church as it reaches out in love to a world in need.

c. God the Holy Spirit

Primary children need to know that the Holy Spirit is a Person who awakens love for God in our hearts. God speaks to us today through His Holy Spirit. The Holy Spirit puts our teaching to work in the lives of boys and girls. He takes our words and makes them live for the children. He works in their hearts and enables them to understand and to respond to the gospel. We want to help children become aware of the presence of the Holy Spirit in their lives, and respond in listening and loving obedience.

2. The Primary Child and Salvation

When is a child ready to accept Christ as Saviour? When is he able to comprehend the meaning of salvation? The simplest answer, of course, is when he feels a need—when he becomes aware that he needs a Saviour. This comes at different times and under different circumstances to individual children.

During primary years, as the child becomes increasingly aware of two forces battling within him, we teach about Jesus as Saviour. The primary child is ready to understand the meaning of such verses as:

For God so loved the world, that he gave his only begotten Son, that whosoever believeth in him should not perish, but have everlasting life (John 3:16).

For all have sinned, and come short of the glory of God (Rom. 3:23).

The child who is aware of wrongdoing when he wants to do right, and who feels the weight of unforgiven sins, will understand and welcome the verse: "If we confess our sins, he is faithful and just to forgive us our sins" (1 John 1:9).

In teaching primary children, we hope to lay a firm foundation for accepting Christ. The heart of the gospel is found in the words of Jesus, "That they might know thee the only true God, and Jesus Christ, whom thou hast sent" (John 17:3). God seeks; He freely offers His salvation, but it is up to us to accept. His love calls for personal decision and acceptance.

Do you remember when you came to that moment of decision? Was it a sudden burst of light? "God so loved the world . . . that whosoever . . ." *"Whosoever,* why, that means *me!* God loves *me!* He is seeking *me!* He is offering *me* His salvation. He wants *me* to accept His love and become a new person in Christ Jesus."

In the spiritual growth and development of children, the Holy Spirit seems to have times when He draws in unusual ways. One of these occurs in primary years, particularly for the eight-year-old. We as teachers need to gain skill in leading children to Christ. How can we lead a child to know the joy of salvation? How can this great truth become a part of the child's own experience?

We may talk with the child and explain Bible terms and truths. We use spiritual songs and Bible verses at worship time. Bible stories and other stories that teach salvation truths are helpful. But most importantly, we testify to the wonder of God's redeeming grace in our own lives. We pray especially for the Holy Spirit to make us channels through whom He can speak to children.

Special times should be planned when the child is confronted with a decision to accept Christ as Saviour. The following suggestions may help as you try to lead the children in your group to a time of decision.

"Do you know why Jesus came into the world? He came to help people know that God is loving and always ready to forgive. God sent Jesus into the world to tell us about His love.

"The Bible says, 'God so loved the world, that he gave his only begotten Son, that whosoever believeth in him should not perish, but have everlasting life' (John 3:16).

"The *world*—that means everyone, doesn't it? Yes, that means you and me.

"When God made people, He planned for everyone to be in His family. He planned for everyone to be good and happy. But something sad happened. People turned away from God. They did not obey Him or keep His commandments. But God still loved them. To help them know about His love, God sent Jesus, His Son, into the world. In the loving things Jesus said and did, He showed God's love. At last He died on the Cross so that everyone could come to God and have his sins forgiven. That means that Jesus died for you and for me too. Let's think about it and write the story in our own words." (Write on blackboard or newsprint:)

>God loves us.
>Everyone has sinned.
>God sent Jesus to die for our sins.
>We must be sorry for our sins.
>We must pray and ask God to forgive us.
>God will forgive us.
>He will take us into His family.

We will know that we belong to Him.
We will love and serve Him.

"Shall we read some verses from the Bible?" (Read: John 3:16; Ps. 86:5; Rom. 3:23; John 3:36a.)

"When we come to God in prayer, and ask forgiveness for our sins, He forgives us and saves us from our sins [read 1 John 1:9]. Then we know that we are saved.

"Sometimes God's Holy Spirit whispers to us in our hearts and tells us we need to be saved. Do you feel Him whispering to you right now? Would you like to come and kneel for prayer?" (Sing softly "Lord, I Want to Be a Christian.")

Give opportunity for children to respond but do not pressure them. Depend wholly upon the leadership of the Holy Spirit. This is His work; you are merely the one through whom He can work.

3. The Primary Child and Christian Living

When we accept Christ as Saviour, it makes a difference in how we live. Being a Christian means using our minds, bodies, time, talents, and possessions as God wants us to do. It requires relating to other persons according to Christian values and love. Primary children need to know this. They need to know, too, that we may have fellowship with God through prayer and worship, and may call on Him at any time for help and strength.

Through teaching-learning units and other experiences, primary children should grow in desire to respond to God through loving obedience. They should appreciate the importance of committing their lives to God. They should continue to grow in a sense of personal worth as a child of God, and be able to accept limitations and failures with a wholesome attitude.

Units of study on the Ten Commandments, the teachings of Jesus, and verses from the Epistles are included to help boys and girls know what it means to live as Christians.

4. The Primary Child and the Bible

The Bible is God's authoritative Word through which comes the clear shining of His redemptive love. It tells us what we ought to be and do. Responding to its message brings changes in attitudes and behavior. The Bible tells what God expects of us in regard to our fellowmen. It tells of the Christian hope of final triumph of right over wrong, and eternal life with Christ forever. The Bible gives us a clear picture of the world in which we live today. It helps us fit together the events of life like pieces of a jigsaw puzzle. Bible appreciation units are included in our primary studies. They tell us how God's Word came to us, and present simple facts about Bible structure and organization. Meaningful use of the Bible with primary children includes the telling of Bible stories, simple dramatization, Bible passages and verses for worship and memorization. Passages for choral reading and Bible games are also effective.

5. The Primary Child and the Church

As Christ himself loved the Church, so we as Christian parents and teachers should love the church and share that love with the boys and girls. The church is our strongest ally in communicating the Christian faith. Through the rich fellowship and personal relationships in the church, children are often brought into meaningful relationship with God.

The church offers instruction, inspiration, fellowship, and opportunity for service. Children need its help and its support, and the enrichment that it brings to every phase of living. They should learn to participate in the work and worship of the church, and to have a part in the financial support of God's work.

Units on the Church are a part of our course of study to help us accomplish our objectives.

Primary Bible Studies

The course of study for primary children is made up of teaching-learning units. These units are carefully planned to cover all the stated goals for primary children. Most of the more important emphases appear several times during the course.

What Is a Unit?

A unit is a way of organizing content, materials, and activities around a given subject. It includes purposes, Bible content, devotional materials, and methods of teaching. Ways are given to involve pupils in learning activities through participation intellectually, emotionally, and physically. Purposes are designed that will modify pupils' behavior and help them cope with problems and situations.

A well-planned unit always takes into consideration the needs, abilities, and maturities of the children to be involved in the teaching-learning processes.

A unit of study is like a story, with an introduction, development, climax, and conclusion. The *introduction* tells the children what the unit is about. It begins where the children are, with what they already know and what they would like to know about the subject to be studied. It arouses their interest, and children and teacher alike begin the happy quest for learning. The *development* is the week-by-week unfolding whereby each session contributes to the whole learning experience. The *climax* is the high point of the unit, where the children's interest is keenest, and the materials, activities, and projects are all nearing completion. The *conclusion* is the satisfying portion when questions have been answered as much as possible, and learning activities concluded. The conclusion involves evaluation by the teachers and pupils together.

How long should a unit be? This depends on the subject being studied and the age of the children involved. For primary children the unit should not be shorter than 3 sessions, or longer than 10 sessions. (The one exception that we have made is the continued life of Jesus.)

The strength of a unit lies in the variety of its methods. It offers many possibilities for thinking, problem solving, planning, responsible work habits, thinking of others in terms of Christian living, reading, listening, research, and reporting. The unit also offers opportunity for in-depth study of the subject under consideration. It may be what God is like, what salvation is, what it means to live as friends of Jesus, or how we may share the gospel with others.

The well-planned unit also offers opportunity for individualized instruction through suggesting a variety of activities and materials. It takes into account the differences of children and allows for continuous growth and development at the child's own level of ability.

Before a Unit Begins

When you receive your curriculum materials, you should begin by looking at the unit as a whole. Read the unit introduction first: purposes, Bible content, suggested activities, projects, resources, and supplementary materials. Get a complete picture in your mind of what the unit is all about. Think of the boys and girls you will teach. How do these Bible truths apply to them? What outcomes are most desired? How can you achieve these with your group?

Then try to fit the week-by-week sessions into the whole plan. How does each session help to develop the unit? What activities are best suited to the group? What materials do you need? What activities not listed might be better suited to your group? Will you want to plan any special trips or extra projects with this unit?

Ask yourself these questions: "How can I create interest on the first Sunday? How shall I introduce the unit? What shall we do to involve the children in making plans for our learning quest?"

Suppose your unit of study is on the Church. Will it be practical to take your group on a trip to other areas of the church? If you go to the sanctuary, you could have a discussion first with the children on how to act. What is there about the sanctuary that suggests worship and reverence? While in the sanctuary, have the children go to the organ or piano, and if the musician is available, ask him to talk with the children about the place of the instrument in the worship service. If it seems suitable, have him accompany the children as they sing a song about the church.

Another way to introduce the unit would be with a picture study of different church situations—people singing, praying, Bible reading, and other worship experiences. Sing a song about the church, or tell a story. Then each successive session introduce new songs, poems, pictures, Bible verses, and stories. Invite various church workers or staff members into the Primary Department for a visit (the pastor, the Sunday school superintendent, the caretaker, etc.).

The children could help make a list of questions about the church. Who are the helpers? How can children be helpers?

Evaluate Your Work

After each session, evaluate what has happened. "What did my children gain that will help them understand something of the work and worship of the church? What activities were most enjoyed and helpful? What can we do better next Sunday?"

A more comprehensive evaluation should take place near the end of the unit. Children should be involved in the evaluation, although with younger primaries it should be kept very informal with such questions as, "What did I like about this unit? What new things did I learn? What activities did I like best?"

The teacher may ask himself: "Have changes that we hoped would take place actually happened? What discoveries were made? What new sense of meaning and value has been woven into the thoughts and lives of the children? How much of a sense of personal responsibility in the light of the gospel have they gained?"

If you have a tape recorder, it is helpful to tape a session and later listen to the tape to evaluate what happened.

Teaching Materials in the Primary Course

The Primary Bible Studies course contains the following materials for teachers, parents, and children.

Primary Teacher

The teacher's guide contains units of study for a given quarter. Each unit is planned around a central purpose directly related to our goals and objectives. The session purposes are chosen to help achieve the central purpose. Related Bible stories and verses, other Christian teaching stories, songs, pictures, and activities are woven into each session.

Appropriate learning activities are suggested for each unit from which the teacher may choose those best suited to his particular group of children. Suggestions are given in the sessions for implementing these activities as the unit progresses.

The needs and interests of the children are presented and the teacher alerted to ways these may be met through teaching the unit.

Help is given throughout the unit for the teacher to relate Bible truths to the child's own life needs and experiences.

Ways to use the various curriculum pieces are given and additional resource materials are suggested.

Devotional material and helpful articles on methods and needs of children are also included in *Primary Teacher*.

Primary Bible Stories

This booklet contains Bible stories or stories with Bible background for use at Sunday school and at home. Bible verses, poems, songs, and things to do are included. Full-color and black-and-white Bible and contemporary pictures add meaning and beauty to the booklet.

The booklets are written with the vocabulary and reading ability of the second-grade child in mind. Suggestions for additional use through guided study and in-depth thinking are given in *Primary Teacher*.

Primary Teaching Resources

The teaching packet contains large teaching pictures and *Nu-Vu* build-up stories. Also Bible memory cards, vocabulary cards, posters, puppets, charts, games, build-up or bulletin-board items, and stand-ups are included from time to time.

The *Nu-Vu* build-up pictures of stick-on figures with

backgrounds in full color help the teacher present Bible stories and Christian teachings in more interesting and effective ways. *Nu-Vu* pictures are designed to clarify and enrich the children's understanding of the stories and teachings.

Primary Activities

Activities contains sheets of things to make and do, simple blanks to fill in, and occasionally puzzles. Take-home pieces to encourage family worship, and song charts are included. Additional suggestions are given in *Primary Teacher* to make these activities as creative as possible. Children are encouraged to use their own ideas in a creative way.

Wonder Time

This four-page story paper contains stories, poems, worship thoughts, pictures, puzzles, and ideas for things to do. It enhances the work of the Sunday school session and offers Christian teachings in the child's home and weekday life. Original poems, prayers, and short stories by the children are featured occasionally.

Table Talk

This is a quarterly guide for family worship where there are children in the home. Its basic approach is discussion with parents to reinforce what the children learn at Sunday school. Important concepts covered in Primary Bible Studies provide the background for these discussions. Ideas and truths which children have explored on Sunday are reviewed in depth within the family circle.

Stories, anecdotes, problem situations, and questions are given to help guide the parents through a Bible study. Suggestions are included that involve the whole family in reading, singing, discussing, and praying. Materials which the children bring home are also woven into these worship times together.

A Look at Curriculum Materials

Before we use any curriculum materials with children, we need to know the objectives on which they are based. We need also to ask ourselves these important questions:
1. Are the materials biblically sound?
2. Are they correct doctrinally?
3. Are they based on sound educational procedures and philosophy?
4. Are they planned with the child's needs and development in mind?
5. Are they pupil-centered rather than teacher-centered?
6. Do they take into consideration the whole child: mentally, spiritually, and physically?

How Shall We Group Them?

If you have taught primary boys and girls for any length of time, you realize the wide differences in the skills and maturities of younger and older primaries. The first grader (six years old) is just beginning to read and write. Sometimes it is a slow and painful process to him, although he is bursting with enthusiasm and eagerness to learn. A look at his emotional and physical development also tells us it is a time of rapid change, development, and extreme behavior. He needs curriculum materials that are planned with him in mind.

The second grader (seven years old) is gaining more skill and poise, but he is not yet ready for the challenging work of the third grader. Some second graders read very well and are beginning to think in more concrete terms than the first graders.

The third grader (eight years old) usually reads very well and has learned to write. He is eager to use his skills and is ready for work that challenges him mentally. He is especially interested in more Bible study, thought questions, puzzles, true-and-false statements, and activities which call for more initiative and individualized learning. He is inclined to be bored with materials planned for younger primaries.

The fourth grader (nine years old) is levelling off from a period of rapid development. He is often lost in the Junior Department in work that has been planned to challenge the capable fifth and sixth graders. The fourth grader needs special consideration in the planning of the Sunday school.

Thus the best grouping according to educators is:
1. Primaries, first and second graders
2. Middlers, third and fourth graders
3. Juniors, fifth and sixth graders

Primary Bible Studies curriculum materials are planned for two-year grouping, specifically for children six and seven years of age. We recommend that wherever possible the two-year grouping be adopted. Children in the first and second grades, six and seven years of age, should be grouped as primaries, using primary lesson materials.

Children in the third and fourth grades, eight and nine years of age, should be grouped as middlers, using middler lesson materials.

This text has been prepared for teachers of the primary group, children of first and second grades. However, we have taken into account the local situations where the broader three-year primary grouping is followed. Methods of teaching suitable to both younger and older primaries are presented.

The content of both primary and middler courses has been planned on similar three-year cycles. Thus children progressing through the Sunday school will receive all the important emphases on either primary or middler level.

For Further Study

1. What is an important, long-range goal for teaching primary children?
2. What experiences did you have as a child that made you aware of God? How do the memories of these experiences help you as you plan for your group?
3. Study the unit and session purposes in your current lesson materials. Have you seen any evidences in the children that some of these purposes are being achieved?
4. What do you consider to be your best approach for teaching children about God?

Chapter 4

Creating A Climate for Learning

*There was a child went forth one day
To learn of God.
To the place called the house of God he went, for a certain hour one day in seven.
And that hour became a part of him for all the years stretching ahead.*

—Author Unknown

How Children Learn

Every primary teacher needs to know how children learn, and how to involve the whole child in the learning process. It is important also to help the child form his own ideas and concepts and to discover for himself the meaning of life as it relates to the Christian faith.

If a child is to grow and develop as an individual, and most importantly, as a Christian, he must have experiences that are meaningful to him. This discovery of meaning comes when the child is involved. As teachers we must challenge each child to think, to feel, to act, and to express himself as he learns.

Before learning can take place, however, there must be a readiness to learn. The child must *want* to learn what we are trying to teach. There must be *practice* also—activities and experiences that help the child put into practice what he has learned. Then there must be *satisfaction* with what has been learned. Jesus used these three principles when He taught His disciples. He caught their attention first, and made them ready and eager to hear His words. Then He gave them something practical to do,

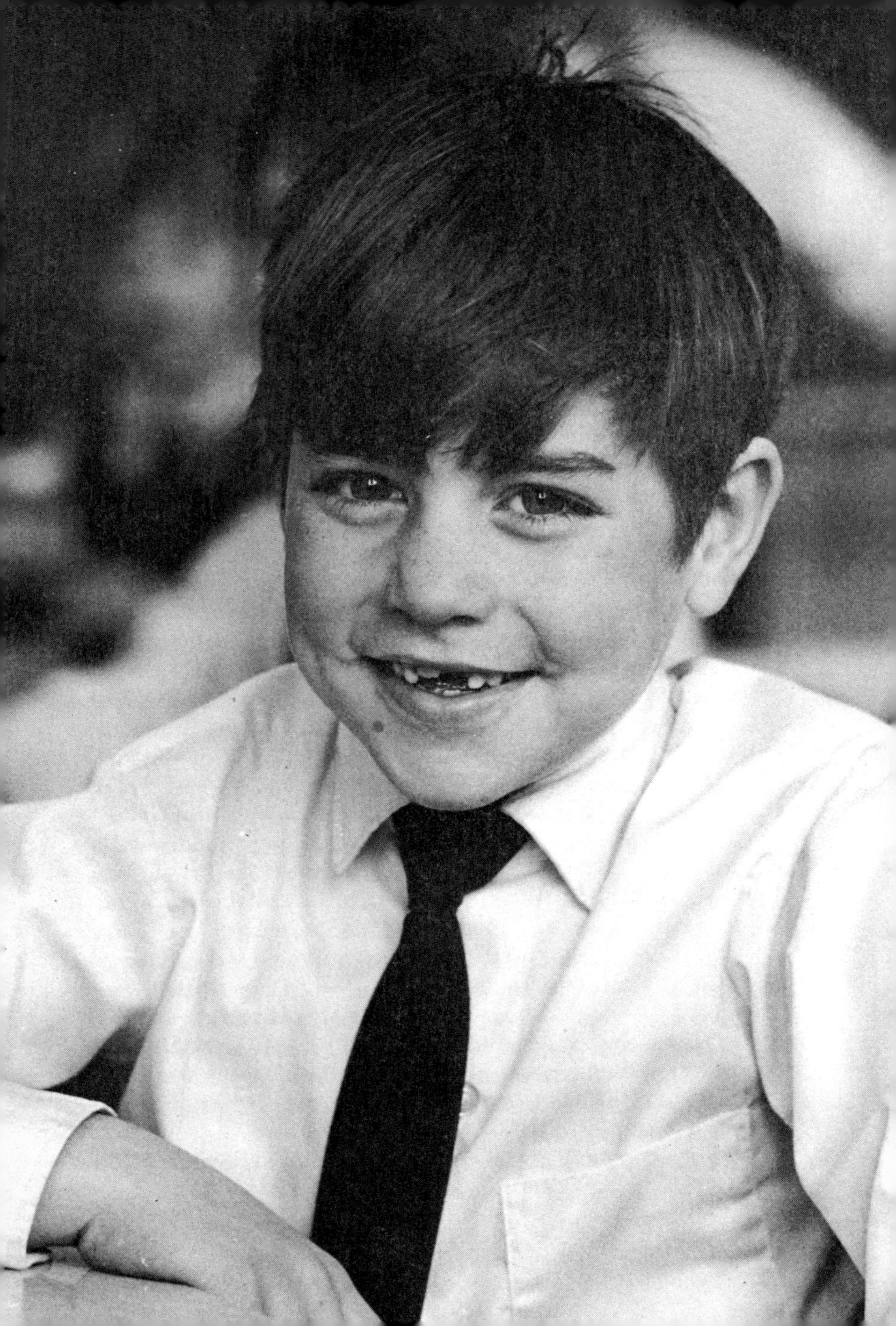

so that they would know the joy and satisfaction that come from doing.

Learning Through Sensory Experiences

One of the important ways in which children learn is through the physical senses: **seeing, hearing, touching, tasting,** and **smelling.** Too often we are concerned only with what children see and hear and do not take advantage of other sensory experiences. Helen Keller, who had to learn everything through her delicate fingertips, urged teachers and parents to teach children through all their senses.

What We See

What a child sees helps him to remember. Visual imagery has something unique to contribute to the learning process quite apart from mere learning of facts. The greatest value of what a child sees is the effect on his emotions. When he is moved by a beautiful picture, a real object, an attractive room, he feels deep inside him what he is learning.

What are some of the seeing experiences a child may have on Sunday morning? First of all, the appearance of the room as he enters. Then the teacher, her friendly smile and warm welcome, her attitude through the whole session. The child sees the gospel according to those who are seeking to interpret its meaning and values.

Other seeing experiences include books, pictures, projected pictures, charts, and posters. Trips to the sanctuary, a visit to a shut-in or to a neighborhood synagogue, a hike on Saturday afternoon, all afford seeing experiences by which a child may perceive and find meaning.

What We Hear

Hearing experiences may include music (singing and

instrumental), stories, poems, conversation, discussion, Bible reading, and prayer. These experiences include the tone of the teacher's voice that denotes her enthusiasm (or lack of it!), her sense of wonder and awe, and her depth of feeling during worship. Record players and tape recorders offer interesting listening experiences.

What We Touch

Touching experiences are important. The child's first impulse when he sees something new and interesting is to reach out and touch it. Objects are to be touched and handled. Pictures should be sturdy enough to be touched as well as looked at. Touch-and-feel materials should be made available for making collages. Children may be encouraged to feel the velvety softness of a rose, the smoothness of a deep red apple. A touch-and-feel game may be played by placing objects in a paper bag, letting the children feel them and guess what each is.

What We Smell

The smell of fresh pine branches and candles at Christmastime adds meaning to experiences at church. The delicate fragrance of spring flowers, the tangy aroma of newly harvested fruits in the fall strengthen the child's faith as he associates these wonders with God's lovingkindness. The sense of smell helps to recall memories perhaps more than any other sense.

What We Taste

The primary children were studying a unit on Abraham. They planned an imaginary birthday party for Isaac, Abraham's son. The children sat in a semicircle on the floor. First there was a time of worship together as they thought of how God called Abraham out of the land of Ur and had given his people a beautiful new country. They recalled how God had promised to give Abraham a son, and now Isaac had come to make Abraham and Sarah happy. The children sang "A Song of Joy," and recalled Bible verses. When refreshment time came, there were little round crackers spread with honey. There were grapes and bits of cheese which reminded them of the kinds of food that Abraham and his family enjoyed. Prayer was offered, thanking God for His goodness.

Making Use of All the Senses

When the Hebrew people taught their children the importance of the Sabbath day, they used all of the senses. First, at twilight, the ram's horn blew, starting the Sabbath (hearing). The people washed their hands, faces, and feet and rubbed their bodies with sweet herbs (smelling). The Sabbath lamps were lit; the mother placed myrtle and olive branches on the low table (seeing). Special food was prepared in advance: freshly baked Sabbath loaves and ripe fruit (smelling, tasting). As the first star of the evening appeared (seeing), the father blessed the mother, and then both parents blessed the children (touching, hearing). The Sabbath meal was eaten with joy and thanksgiving. Prayers and Bible verses expressed gratitude and praise to God. No wonder the children learned in unforgettable ways of the goodness and wonder of God's love!

Learning Through Curiosity

Anything which arouses a child's curiosity and makes him eager to learn is important. It may be a question, a poem, an object, a picture, anything which causes the child to wonder. These may be used to introduce a story, a new song, a research project, or a creative activity such as writing, drawing, or painting.

Learning Through Association

When we relate what we want to teach to what a child already knows, we are using sound educational methods. If new experiences are to have meaning for boys and girls, they must be able to relate the new learning to what they already know and feel. Teachers must consider experiences children have had or are having in order to plan for effective learning.

Learning Through Variety

A child learns through a variety of methods. Children do not all learn alike or at the same rate. What appeals to one child may not appeal to another. The creative teacher uses a variety of methods. The children too may often have a part in choosing the methods to be used, such as whether to dramatize a story, pose pictures, make a mural or frieze, or make a scrapbook for a child who is ill.

Learning Through Imitation

A child imitates what he sees. He becomes the character he sees on television or reads about in a book. He imitates the grown-ups around him in the home, at school, and at church. This love of acting out another person makes dramatic play, role playing, and picture posing important tools in teaching. Children form attitudes, values, and standards by imitating those around them.

Learning Through Insight

What is it that helps a child learn and understand spiritual truths beyond his years? What helps him to say suddenly, "Oh, I get it," or, "Oh, I see"? God has given him that quality of spirit that helps him respond to spiritual truths. If you have taught children for a while, no doubt you have been amazed at some of their answers (as well as their questions!). The Holy Spirit uses this spiritual insight to give meaning and understanding to what we try to teach.

One day Jesus put a child in the midst of grown-ups, and said, "Except ye . . . become as little children, ye shall not enter into the kingdom of heaven" (Matt. 18:3). Perhaps He had in mind their spiritual insight.

Where Primary Children Meet

The primary child's physical environment on Sunday morning is important to the way he feels and the way he responds to Christian teaching. Where children meet may largely determine what they learn. Rooms that are adequate in space, orderly, and attractive in appearance will greatly enrich the child's learning experience.

A good environment includes all the external influences that affect children.

If your church is planning a new building, or the remodeling of present facilities, a careful study should be made of the needs of primary children. Appoint a committee to confer with the architect in the planning stages of any building project. Remember to build for the years ahead as well as for today. Consider the present trends in education and do not build so that you hinder teaching 10 or 20 years from now.

In making these plans, the child's basic needs should be considered. The ways children learn are also important. How can the space and equipment help to meet these needs?

How Much Space?

In planning space for primary children, we remind ourselves that Christian education is more than the teaching of facts. Children learn more effectively through a rich environment and a wide variety of experiences. Methods of teaching and facilities go together. Teaching-learning experiences where children become actively involved require space. Children need to move about; to work together for dramatization, role playing, art activities, music, and worship. Rooms often determine for or against participation by the children.

An overcrowded room may cause discipline problems. When children feel fenced in, something is bound to happen—and it is usually not the best. Overcrowding results in tension and fatigue.

In planning for open-room teaching, there should be at least 25 square feet of space for each child. This allows for needed activities in small groups, and space for worship when the whole group meets together.

If in your church you have the primary assembly room and small classrooms adjacent with no hope of building or remodeling soon, see what can be done to make some changes. Are there partitions that could be removed? Can you take out superfluous furniture—an oversized piano, or extra chairs or tables? Each child needs only one chair. Children are accustomed to carrying chairs from place to place in public school and can do so quietly and with little confusion. With extra space in the assembly room, can you move one or more groups from the small classrooms into the larger one? Can you remove doors to give a feeling of openness?

It may appear at first that open-room teaching requires more space than the assembly and classroom plan. However, it is actually an economy to plan rooms with flexible use rather than a setup for one use only. There is also a saving in space when partitions and walls are eliminated.

Location. Usually the best place for the primary room

or department is on the ground level. South and east exposures are usually preferred. Rest-room facilities and a drinking fountain at proper height should be readily accessible.

Windows. These should be at proper level for children to see out. It is most desirable where possible for the children to look out on an open court or lawn with trees, and flowers in season. Wide windowsills are preferred. The window area should equal 20 to 30 percent of the floor area. However, provision should also be made for darkening the room in order to use audiovisual equipment successfully.

Floors. The floor covering should be durable and attractive. Several suitable coverings are now on the market. Perhaps the most satisfactory is carpeting. It is attractive and eliminates noise. It is more economical to keep up than waxed tile or wood floors. Carpeting is comfortable and inviting too when children have activities that call for sitting on the floor.

Storage. Adequate storage space should be provided. Some of the cabinets should be placed low enough for the children to put away their own materials. Provision should be made for filing pictures, song charts, and audiovisual equipment. A coatrack of proper height should be provided for children's wraps.

In a warm climate, plans should include air conditioning. Children and teachers cannot work and worship effectively when they are too uncomfortable.

Walls. The color on the walls is important. A light, pastel shade is best. If your room is on the east side with plenty of morning sun, choose a soft green or blue. In darker rooms, use shades of yellow, peach, or soft rose.

On one wall, plan for a tack board 30 inches from the floor, where the children may display their work and add beauty and interest to the room. Include a picture rail, also 30 inches from the floor.

Tables and chairs. The best chair for primary children is 14 inches from the floor. The tables should be 10 inches higher than the chairs. Rectangular tables 30" x 60" are best. A small Bible table and a reading table will also be needed.

A small upright piano is ideal. If you do not have a suitable piano, however, consider using an autoharp, record player, or melody bells instead.

In addition to walls and furniture, the room itself must speak of interesting things. It must open up new ideas and beckon the children to discover, explore, create, and evaluate. The room should reflect the interests of the group and the current season or subject. It must belong uniquely to the group that meets there. A chart with ongoing plans or questions listed, pictures, objects, and creative work all serve to develop and sustain interest.

The imaginative teacher can make any meeting area interesting even if it be only a corner behind the piano, the church kitchen, or rear pews of the sanctuary.

The children need ready access to resource materials, books, recordings, Bibles, objects, charts, a Bible dictionary, tape recorder, View-master, or Show 'N Tell.

The shelves or cabinets should contain art supplies, paper, and other materials for making and doing.

Team Teaching

Team teaching is a shared experience of teaching-learning. It is when two or more adults join together to plan, study, pray, teach, and learn from one another. The children also may become members of the team as they are involved in some of the planning and in the teaching-learning process.

Each adult member of the team attends and participates in all the planning meetings and in the teaching sessions. As in all good teaching, plans are flexible enough so that children may have a part in choosing, evaluating, and helping to carry out the activities.

Why Team Teaching?

What are the advantages of team teaching? Why are those who have tried it enthusiastic about the results?

In team teaching children have the advantage of the skills and insights of several teachers instead of one. They are exposed also to several warmhearted, concerned teachers. Enthusiasm is catching, and one enthusiastic teacher may spark the entire group.

Aids Teacher Recruitment

With the team-teaching system, teaching can become a training and learn-as-you-go process for beginning workers. New teachers have opportunity to develop skills and learn proper methods as they plan and work with veteran teachers. Inexperienced teachers are more willing to share responsibilities than to take full charge. Men who enjoy being with children but who feel limited in teaching experience will often be willing to join a team. Later as they gain confidence and knowledge they feel better able to take on fuller responsibilities.

Provides Greater Opportunity for Discovery Learning

In team teaching there is apt to be greater opportunity for questions, thinking, exploring, and increased learning in depth. Children are helped to discover meaning and value for themselves. As teachers plan together and learn from one another, discovery-learning is more likely to occur. One teacher with insight and ability to encourage children to think may help to develop an atmosphere for creative thinking and planning. This may inspire other teachers to be creative and say to the child, "Let's find out." Thus the Christian faith is more likely to become the child's own as he thinks and discovers some of the answers for himself.

How Does Team Teaching Work?

One teacher on the team becomes the lead teacher. He is responsible for planning sessions, and usually takes charge of the larger group on Sunday. The other responsibilities are shared by the adult team members. This would include music experiences, storytelling, and supervision of small-group or individual activities.

Planning sessions by the team should be held weekly. Perhaps an hour before midweek or Sunday evening service will be best, or an evening in a teacher's home may be preferred. Whenever you plan together, begin and end your meetings on time. If a weekly meeting is impossible, meet at least once a month and before each new unit.

A Prayer Partner on the Team

A special prayer partner may be a most valuable and loved member of the team. This could be an older person in the church, perhaps one who can no longer serve as a regular teacher but who loves children and knows how to pray effectively. The prayer partner should come into the group on Sunday morning to become acquainted with the teachers and children and to share in their concerns and interests. He is alerted to special needs and these become definite prayer requests. Such a person can add much to the fellowship and ministry of the Sunday school department.

When Children Worship

In simple terms we may say that worship is feeling near to God, and responding to Him in love and praise. Worship means active fellowship with God. With children it may be a fleeting moment of ecstasy when a child says, "Oh, I just love God!" Or it may be a time of quietness when teacher and child alike feel His loving presence.

Worship is woven into all we do on Sunday morning. Our planning together, our music, activities, storytelling, conversation—whatever we do we want children to feel near to God and be brought into active fellowship with Him. Planned times of worship should be an outgrowth of the children's experiences in presession or in the class.

When planning worship with children, two practical aspects are important: *atmosphere* and *participation*.

The environment can add to or detract from worship. Children are most sensitive to their surroundings. A comfortable, well-lighted room, pleasing to look at, is conducive to worship. Creating a spirit of worship is an added dimension. Care must be given to select the right pictures, songs, and objects to be used.

The Teacher and Worship

The teacher's attitude and spirit are most important in creating this mood for worship. If he is impersonal, too hurried, nervous, or poorly prepared, the children are quick to sense this. When he comes before the children serene, joyful, and reverent, it makes a difference. If he is to help create an atmosphere for worship, he himself must truly worship.

The Children's Participation

Participation by the children in the planning and

preparation is important. They may help to plan the interest center. The Bible is always central but we may change other things to help create atmosphere. Something the children have made—a picture, poem, or short story they have written—makes worship more meaningful. A group prayer worked out by them, sometimes in a smaller group, may be used by the entire assembly. Song charts the children have illustrated, or pictures they have drawn to lift up important ideas in a song, have meaning. A tape recording of a choral reading, a favorite Bible story dramatized, a picture posed, all may be worshipful. Thus the worship time becomes one that belongs to the children themselves.

Experiences That Lead to Worship

Experience is the basis of true worship. Experiences of awe, wonder, joy, thankfulness, praise, and purpose, all must come from the depths of the teacher's own feelings as well as those of the children if they are to truly worship together.

What can we do to create a sense of wonder? Three things lead to it: *something new, something beautiful,* and *something mysterious.* The teacher may plan to have one or even all three in order to help the children wonder. It may be a new picture, a beautiful plant or bouquet of real flowers at the Bible center. Objects from the out-of-doors may arouse interest and wonder. What is more mysterious than a gray cocoon where a moth or butterfly sleeps within during the winter months? A milkweed pod, a bird's nest, a shell on the table add mystery. A Bible verse, "The earth is full of thy riches," brings a mood of worship. Any experiences that help children learn more about God the Creator and Sustainer lead them to sense the wonder of life and growth, and the orderly plan of our world.

Wonder comes too from studying the Bible and exploring its beauty and truth. Think of the wonder of the gospel, the good news of the Bible:

For God so loved the world (the wonder of His love),
that he gave (the wonder of His giving)
his only begotten Son (the wonder of the Gift—the Lord Jesus),
that whosoever (that takes each of us in)
believeth in him (the wonder of faith)
should not perish, but have everlasting life (the wonder of life eternal, begun now and continued with Him forever).

Wonder and awe come as teacher and children explore passages of the Bible together and think of the greatness and majesty of God.

The Bible also provides language for worship:
Sing to the Lord a new song,
for He has done wonderful things (Ps. 98:1, NASB).
O Lord, how many are Thy works!
In wisdom Thou hast made them all (Ps. 104:24, NASB).

We need to lead children into experiences of joy in worship. This can happen only if the teacher feels joy in her own heart—the joy of loving and serving God and being filled with the Holy Spirit.

We want children to know the joy of serving the Lord. Our Christian faith is not something static or dead; it is radiant, alive, and full of joy. The Apostle Peter wrote of "joy unspeakable and full of glory." That joy can be ours to share as we love and serve God.

Joyful singing, joyful passages from the Bible, joy in our hearts that finds expression through our voices, our faces, and our testimonies—the children can see, feel, and share this joy.

Children may also worship in the joyful and loving atmosphere of planning for a visit to a shut-in or a child who is ill.

Creating a Prayer for Worship

The fall days were crisp and sunny. The leaves on the trees were changing to shades of red, gold, and yellow. As the children came to Sunday school, they were aware of the beauty around them.

"Now would be a good time to write a thank-You prayer to God," a lead teacher said to her assistant. "Would you help the children compose one for our worship time?"

"I'll try," said the assistant.

When they met in the large group that morning, the teacher discussed the activity with them. First they talked about the beauty of the fall season. Some of the children had found books at the book center that had been opened (on purpose) to beautiful pictures and poems. Others had drawn pictures at the art center. Still others had enjoyed some objects at the wonder center. And many remembered the colorful leaves they had seen on the way to Sunday school.

The teacher asked, "Would you like to write a prayer poem thanking God for some of the wonders of fall?"

As the children responded, she wrote down a list of things they suggested: leaves, flowers, pumpkins, moon, and apples.

"Next Saturday we will have a walk in the woods," the teacher said. "Perhaps you will see some things to add to this list before we write our prayer poem."

The next Saturday the teachers and children met for a

walk in a nearby park. Each child was given a large paper bag for collecting treasures, and they set off for a happy walk in the woods. They came back by noon with their sacks filled with acorns, seedpods, leaves, berries, and dried flowers.

A picnic lunch around a campfire was the high point of the outing. As the children gathered around, the sunlight sifted through the autumn trees and sparkled on the water of a small lake nearby. A teacher led the group in singing "God, Who Made the World of Beauty." Prayer was offered for the food and for the beauty of God's world.

The next day the children brought many of their treasures to Sunday school with them to help relive the happy experience. And there were many things to add to the list for the prayer poem: seedpods, berries, sunshine, the lake, and the campfire. The teacher helped them to form their thoughts into simple sentences. There was no need for rhyming, for that would have spoiled it. The children chose a simple response, "We thank You," for each stanza:

>*For the beauty in the fall,*
>*For the leaves and for the flowers,*
>*We thank You.*
>
>*For the moon that shines above,*
>*For the apples and the pumpkins,*
>*We thank You.*
>
>*For so many things to see,*
>*For the seedpods and the berries,*
>*We thank You.*
>
>*For the sunlight through the trees,*
>*For the lake with shining water,*
>*We thank You.*
>
>*For the campfires burning bright,*

*For our homes and rest at night,
We thank You.*

When the prayer poem was complete and the children used it responsively in their worship time, God seemed very near to them and to the teachers as well.

Later a large scrapbook was made, and pictures cut out to illustrate the prayer poem. This was placed on the reading table to be enjoyed during the entire fall season.

Helping Children to Pray

Young children usually learn to pray quite naturally in the Christian home. "Thank You, God, for my food"; "Thank You for my bed"; "Thank You for Mommie and Daddy"; "Help me to be good." These are all a part of the child's first responses to God. Sometimes simple prayers are memorized and used to help a child express his own thoughts and feelings to God.

As children grow spiritually, they need to develop in their concept and practice of prayer. How can we help them realize the need for and the privilege of this fellowship with God? First, they learn to pray as they sense the quality of our prayer lives, as we pray with them and for them in earnestness and simplicity. If God is real to us, if the experience of prayer is meaningful, we can convey this reality to the boys and girls. If we pray humbly, simply, and expectantly, children will be led to do likewise.

Children need help in expressing their feelings and needs to God. At times it is wise to ask them to mention things for which they wish to thank God, or needs they may have: a sick parent or schoolmate, a problem in the family. A teacher may pray, mentioning all concerns that have been suggested. Sometimes the children, as they grow and develop confidence, are willing to lead in prayer. The Lord's Prayer may be used as a group prayer.

We must help children understand that prayer is listening as well as speaking. And they need to know that true prayer involves commitment to God's will.

Primaries need to realize that they can pray anytime, anywhere, and that God is always ready to hear and answer. Prayers for forgiveness, for courage, for our country, and for world needs are to be encouraged. When children hear of needs in other parts of the world—war, hunger, or disaster—they are moved to compassion. It helps them to express these concerns to God and to have the confidence that "effectual fervent prayer . . . availeth much."

For Further Study

1. Plan to spend some time in your primary room. Make a list of the ways the room is planned for teaching-learning experiences. Can it be improved?

2. What sensory experiences have you used lately in your teaching? Describe what happened.

3. If you visit a primary room and see few pictures on display, no work of the children in evidence, no reading table, wonder center, or other interest centers, what kind of teaching situation probably exists?

4. What can you plan for next Sunday that will help the children have a sense of wonder?

5. If you do team teaching, work out a plan for your next meeting with the team. How will the various responsibilities be shared?

Chapter 5

Let's Be Creative

And God said, Let us make man in our image.
—Gen. 1:26

Created in the image of God. What does that say to us as teachers of children? Doesn't it tell us that God has planned for us to be creative also as we share His redemptive love with those whom we teach?

But what do we mean when we say *creative?* And how can we become more creative in teaching the Bible and related Christian truths to boys and girls? Being creative involves using our own intellectual powers and imagination—that special something with which we were born and which belongs uniquely to each of us. It means that we have ideas in addition to the printed materials placed in our hands. We think of our particular group of children and use originality to adapt the lesson materials to fit the needs of the group and individual children.

When we feel comfortable with our plans and methods, we have a sense of joy as we come before the children. Then we are enthusiastic, and inspire our children to be likewise. When the teacher meets with the children in a happy, relaxed manner, they will respond, and a learning environment is created for both teacher and pupils. The teacher has respect for the children, for their ideas and for what they can do. He encourages them to express ideas and to work them out creatively. He does not expect or exact perfection.

Wasn't this the way that Jesus taught? He used objects and materials at hand to capture the attention of His listeners. He involved them in the learning process by asking questions and listening to them. He had the highest

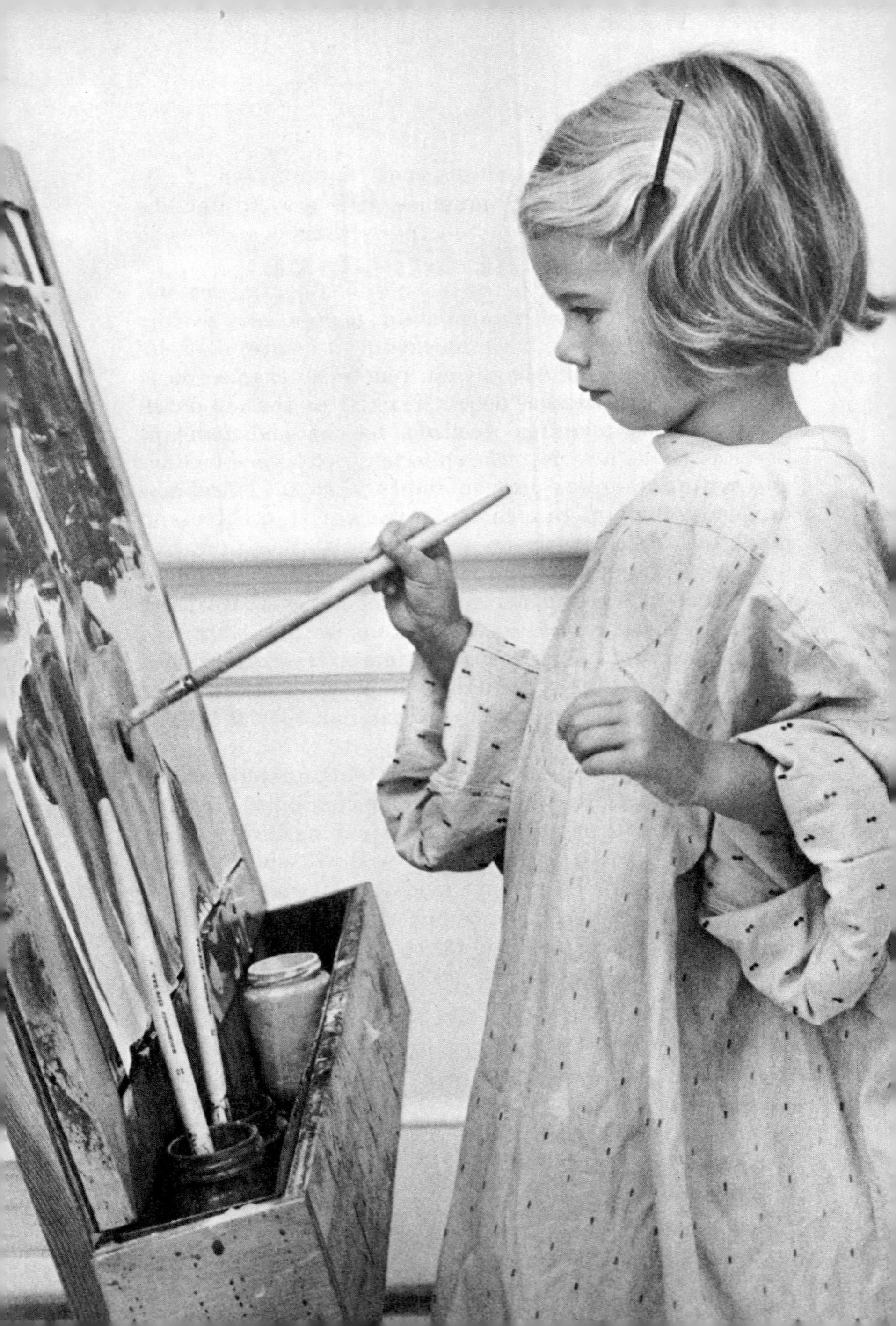

respect for children and always took time for them. Children felt at home in His presence. It is easy to imagine that He encouraged them to express their own ideas to Him.

Creative teaching helps to build self-confidence and courage in the shy, withdrawn child. It provides a worthy outlet for the restless, boisterous child. It creates a wholesome atmosphere for friendly working together as a group.

Creative expression helps the child to develop on all three levels of learning: *knowing, feeling,* and *doing.* It develops the mind, helps the child to express inner feelings and attitudes, and to grow in ability to make choices and decisions. It helps him to find solutions to problems in everyday living.

Creative teaching and learning helps children to think, feel, plan, carry out, appreciate, and evaluate. Each of these steps is important if a child is to truly learn.

But you say, "I am not a very creative person. I have little confidence in my own ideas. I am timid about trying new things with my children. How can I change? Where do I begin?"

The sincere teacher begins first by claiming his freedom to develop his creative powers as a child of God and a co-worker with Him. What higher calling is there than this? Then the teacher prays that God will open his eyes and illuminate his mind as he reads, studies, and plans for his class. With this assurance and with the Holy Spirit as Guide, he turns to planning for the next unit or the next session in a creative way.

Study Your Materials

The teacher should ask first, "What are the purposes for the unit? For the session? How do these purposes apply to my group? What purpose is most needed and most likely to be accomplished?"

Next, he studies the Bible material and Bible background. He makes use of a good Bible dictionary and Bible concordance. He asks, "What does the Bible say to me as a follower of Christ? What should this session mean to the children I teach? What suggested activities will help me accomplish the purposes? How can I enrich these activities or think of others that are better suited to my group?"

The teacher then studies the planned visual aids: pictures, posters, or charts, and asks himself, "How can these be used so that they will have real meaning for the children? What other poems, pictures, or objects can I use that will enrich the session? How can the children themselves be involved in the teaching-learning experiences?

"What songs and other music will help the children understand and feel the truth of today's session? What can I do to lead them into moments of worship?

"What pictures or objects will enrich the Bible story? What questions can I use to help the boys and girls evaluate what we have learned together? How can I get the most effective use from the pupil books?"

When you have decided that a certain procedure would be helpful, prepare carefully for it. If your plans call for making collages, make one yourself at home. If you expect to use puppets, experiment with making one at home before you try to help the children make them.

When the Children Come

When the children first arrive, they are eager and alert, ready to go. The teacher should capture their interest and attention at once, involving them in activities that require their best thinking and abilities. You must determine whether you should tell the Bible story early in the session or use this prime time for research or making reports. Ask yourself when is the best time for art activities, or Bible games, or discussions.

The effective teacher varies methods during the hour. If the early part of the session involves listening (a story, recording, tape, or other listening experience), the latter part may involve visual activities such as looking at pictures and objects, or drawing pictures.

Individualized Instruction

In public education individualized instruction means extra activities and projects which encourage the child to work independently at his own pace. It includes programmed learning. Materials for these activities may include books, pictures, filmstrips, tape recorders, and View-masters. Special interest centers may include materials for creative writing or art. Science centers are also helpful. This type of learning is particularly suited to third graders or older.

But what about the primary child in the Sunday school? Can there be some attempt at individualized learning in the limited time and resources available to us? The answer is *yes* when the interested teacher is willing and/or able to give the time and effort necessary to thus enrich his teaching.

It is almost impossible for any centrally planned curriculum to include all of the special materials needed for individualized instruction. However, the regular materials suggest many more activities than can be used during the teaching period. The teacher can adapt some of these unused procedures for individual learning experiences. Enrichment materials are also suggested each week which may be made available at reading or other learning centers.

Some children will complete activities in the workbook more quickly than others. The child who finishes early may spend his time at the learning centers in activities that particularly appeal to him.

There should always be books for the children to enjoy and study. If there is no church library, the primary teachers should request books for their department or class. Tape recorders, record players, Show 'N Tell and Viewmasters all give children opportunity for independent learning.

We do not expect every child to learn at the same pace. Nor do children have the same talents and interest. All the needs and interests of the children should be taken into consideration as we plan for our group.

Music centers, art centers, and reading and writing centers all offer opportunities for each child to find his place of interest during presession or extra class time. A nature center with objects to see, feel, touch, and smell may open up a whole new world for a child. A magnifying glass lends added attraction.

Mike has been brought in through the bus ministry. He has little knowledge of the Bible. He does not enjoy music or art. But Mike likes puzzles and Bible games. He can be helped to catch up on Bible knowledge through these activities.

Renee may like to express her feelings through drawing a picture. Jon does not like to draw, but he enjoys playing the autoharp or rhythm instruments. Alice likes dramatic play, but Jeff prefers a book.

Primary children enjoy doing work at home to bring on Sunday to share with the group. Perhaps Jeff would read a book during the week and tell the class about it later. Renee may be asked to draw a picture of something in God's world and bring it to the class. Jon may be permitted on occasion to take the autoharp home during the week and practice an accompaniment to one of the current songs.

Creative Storytelling

Storytelling is an effective means of communication with children. It is often a determining factor in helping to form Christian attitudes and behavior. A good story helps to develop the whole child. It informs, enlightens, and clarifies concepts. It may arouse feelings, and develop attitudes, and motivate conduct. It may help the child to make wise choices and decisions. The right story may help a child to feel at home with people of other lands and races.

The primary age is the age of action and imagination. Children are interested in stories about other children and things they do, problems they face, and how they solve them.

Nature stories also have an appeal for children, but they should be realistic. Stories which depict animals behaving in unnatural ways are not best for primary children.

Stories of Bible people and other heroes of the Christian faith appeal to boys and girls.

A good story gives children insight into spiritual values and helps them set standards for their own lives. A story often leads to moments of worship, or prepares for an experience such as a trip to the sanctuary or to the out-of-doors. Stories may also help children to see the need of a Saviour and bring them to the moment of commitment.

Good storytelling enhances a story much as a lovely frame brings out the beauty of a picture. Prepare your story carefully before you tell it to the children. First read it through thoughtfully and analyze it. What about its structure? How does it begin? What problem or problems does it present? Where does it go from there? What is the step-by-step development? Where is the climax? Does it have a satisfactory conclusion? Will all the questions in the minds of the children be answered?

After you see the story as a whole, live with the characters until they become real to you. Think of the events of the story as a set of slides one after another. What comes first? What follows? As you approach the climax, let your voice indicate this and build up interest.

When you have the story well in mind, practice telling it to someone. You may need to imagine your audience. One primary teacher put the pictures of her husband and two sons on the sofa in front of her as she practiced her story. She knew if she pleased this discriminating audience, she would be successful with the children! And she was.

Excellent rapport with the children made another teacher on the team the favorite storyteller. When it was her turn to tell the story, the children sat forward in their chairs and said, "Oh, good, it's Miss Anderson's turn today." Miss Anderson's love for the children and her interest in all that concerned them helped her to communicate with them in an unusual way.

As a storyteller you may enrich your story by using pictures and objects at the right moment.

A missionary from India was asked to tell a story to a group of primary children. She came before them with her large purse in her hand. That seemed strange and the children wondered about it.

The missionary began by saying, "What do you suppose I have in my purse?" Immediately she had their attention and she waited for their response. After they had made several suggestions, she said, "I have my dress in my purse." She took out a *sari* and put it on before the delighted children. Then she went into an appealing story of a little girl in India who had no parents. She was hungry and needed love and care. The missionary led the children through a simple but moving story of a little girl with whom they could relate. There was no extreme sentimentalism, but the story was told with such sincerity and depth of feeling that the children were with her every moment.

This storyteller began with something familiar (the purse). She aroused curiosity and then went into a story with which the children could identify. She led up to the climax and concluded without moralizing. The story carried its own message and the children understood.

When you tell a story to children, use crisp, colorful words that have meaning for them. Remember the value of repetition and sound effects especially for younger primaries. Change the pitch and color of your voice frequently. Children listen better if your voice is not too loud.

Use direct discourse instead of long descriptive sentences. And don't tell too much; let the children use their imaginations.

Try to be relaxed and natural in your manner. Avoid talking down to the children. Keep eye contact with them as much as possible.

If you prefer to read a story instead of telling it, be thoroughly familiar with the content, so that you can lift your eyes frequently as you read.

When you prepare to tell a Bible story, read it as it is written in your lesson materials; then directly from the Bible. Lesson writers often add details to help clarify meanings for the children; they try not to distort meaning or give wrong interpretations of Bible truths. You will also find it helpful to have one or more good books of Bible stories. Refer to them to see how other writers have told the story. This may help you add interesting details.

What about contemporary stories that illustrate Bible truths? These are valuable and should be a part of teaching procedure. The creative teacher will have books of stories and keep a file of stories clipped from Sunday school papers and other sources.

The open-end story is a variation in teaching procedure. The story revolves around a problem; it has an introduction, development, and climax, but the problem is not solved. The children are asked to suggest possible endings.

Nu-Vu Stories

Nu-Vu stories are visually built up. They are a valuable part of the curriculum. These stories are planned in two to four scenes with suitable backgrounds and figures to represent characters and properties. The figures are placed on the board (background) as the story progresses. The children may later be asked to retell the stories and place the figures themselves. Or one child may tell the story while another places the figures.

Puppets

Puppets add a creative dimension to storytelling, and are widely used in both public school and Sunday school. The teacher may use puppets to represent different characters, and let them speak directly to the class. Children enjoy making puppets and using them in retelling stories.

Puppets are also excellent tools to help a child express his thoughts and feelings. The puppet can do things a child feels too shy or inhibited to do. The child with emotional problems often finds release and satisfaction through the use of puppets. He can act out and identify with the type of person he would like to be. The use of puppets may help him deal with problems for which he sees no solution in real life. Their use also encourages children to work with others in friendly, helpful ways. As children reveal their feelings and problems through the use of puppets, it helps teachers become better acquainted with their pupils and understand their needs.

Many different kinds of puppets may be used: papier-maché, stick puppets, finger puppets, sack puppets, box puppets, plastic- or wooden-spoon puppets.

Puppets are sometimes included in *Primary Teaching Resources*. At other times instructions for making and using them are included in lesson materials. Additional help may be obtained by referring to books on crafts and art activities.

Creative Use of Poetry

Someone has said that poetry is made up of words that have always liked each other but have never gotten together before. Poetry is a song in words. The poet stirs our imagination by talking very little and saying much. The poet makes you see what he sees and feel what he feels. Poetry runs, skips, soars, and flies. Do you see why it helps us in teaching children, to stir imagination, convey feelings, and leave lasting impressions?

There are many ways to use poetry. The right poem may be used to catch attention and open discussion. It may be used to change attitudes and develop a sense of humor. It may help to create a sense of wonder and lead to worship.

The right poem may relieve tensions and create a new atmosphere. Poems help children feel near to God.

I'M GLAD, DEAR GOD

*I'm glad, dear God, You made the day
With happy hours to run and play;
I'm glad You made the nighttime too,
When silver stars come shining through.*

*I'm glad, dear God, for everything
That You have made: the birds that sing,
The soft, white clouds, the sky so blue;
And, oh, I'm glad You made me too!*

An appreciation for poetry leads to enjoyment of Bible poetry. "Let's find a poem in the Bible that tells about God's wonderful world," the teacher may say as she turns to the Psalms and reads selections to the children.

How can you use poems most effectively? Look over your plans for the unit you are now studying and ask yourself, "Will a poem fit here? Will it be more effective if I memorize it?"

Poems are effective in helping clarify meanings of Bible verses. They add interest and meaning to pictures. Poetry provides a good listening experience for children (see Chapter 6). Enjoyable activities may be planned by using poems in making booklets and posters. The children may choose a poem from your file to use in worship or fellowship time. Short poems are usually best. Children may lose interest when the poem is too long.

Creative Writing with Children

A good rule to follow in creative writing with children is to learn to listen to what they say and how they say it. If possible, write their words down just as they say them. A parent has great opportunity to listen to children as they express themselves creatively. One mother overheard her seven-year-old discussing God's love with his older sister. "Of course God loves us," he said. "He made us, didn't He?"

This happens sometimes as children play or as the family rides along in a car. Sometimes a young child makes up a song or poem spontaneously. This should be recorded if possible and the child encouraged to draw pictures to illustrate it.

The Sunday school teacher should also be alert to spontaneous creations from the children, and provide materials and encouragement for further efforts along this line.

Children must have experiences if they are to create. They do not create out of a vacuum. When they hear what other children have written, it helps them to write their own thoughts. Thus prayers, poems, and stories written by children and included in the pupil's "take home" paper occasionally should be read and discussed. Pictures, objects, experiences such as trips out of doors, or looking out a window may spark a brief story.

When the children come on Sunday morning, be prepared with attractive books, pictures, or objects. Show the children an interesting picture. Give them opportunity to express themselves or to answer questions about what they see in the picture. Let them tell what they think might be happening. Write down their ideas and comments on a large sheet of paper. Let them choose a title such as "What Our Picture Tells Us." Put it up on the bulletin board or on the wall.

Another interesting activity is to have the children write a report of a trip. Seven-year-old Susan went calling with her mother. Later she expressed her feelings in a poem to share with her class at Sunday school.

Sunday

Birds are singing;
Bells are ringing.
A day of cheer!
Sunday is here.

Children are calling
Others to come,
To hear the story
Of God's holy Son.

Let the children discuss what they would like to tell about a trip. Older children can write down their ideas. With younger children the teacher will need to record their thoughts. Trying to write or spell sometimes causes a child to lose his creative spark.

In group writing, sometimes one creative child can spark the entire group into writing a poem or prayer for use in the worship time.

Children may be encouraged to write letters to children of missionaries, notes to shut-ins or absentees, or thank-you letters to church workers or other resource persons who have visited them. They may write brief stories to go with printed pictures or their own drawings. They may also help to write open-end stories for role playing.

Mindy wrote a short essay about her father.

Who Is My Father?

My father is someone who loves me and cares for me. My father is a kind father. I love my father.

Mark, a second grader, wrote this poem:

March Wind

The March wind tosses the branches to and fro.
It sweeps the walk and twirls the sailboats in the sea.
It blows my paper and softly whispers through the trees.

Joel, age eight, wrote the following Christmas poem:

I am glad
For Christmas Day;
Jesus was born
That morn.
Shepherds found where
He lay;
Wise men came from
Far away,
And worshiped Him.

Haiku Poetry

Children enjoy writing the Japanese form of poetry called haiku. This simple poem has 17 syllables, with three lines, as follows:

first line, five syllables
second line, seven syllables
third line, five syllables

The first line tells *when* or *why*, the second line *where*, and the third line *how* or *what*. It is usually about nature but may be used in this way:

PALM SUNDAY
On a happy day
Going to Jerusalem
Children sang praises.

JESUS
A long time ago
Upon a grassy hillside
Jesus taught people.

THE STORM
On a stormy night
Winds were high on Galilee,
Jesus said, "Be still."

First-grade children can be helped to write simple prayers. The teacher may start by writing the words: "Thank You, God, for . . . ," and let the children suggest what to add. They should be helped to think of descriptive words. Sometimes the children may fill in a rebus by drawing pictures of things for which they are thankful.

A second grade class wrote this:

A Springtime Prayer

Thank You, God, for (birds) *and* (flowers),*
For (sun) *and* (rain),
(Butterflies) *and* (seeds).
Thank You, God.

For Further Study

1. Study the lesson materials you are now using. What creative activities are best suited to your group? Perhaps you can think of a better activity; describe it and tell why you think it is better.

2. Find a suitable poem to use with your group. What picture or object can you use to enhance its value? Make a puppet to use with a contemporary story and tell how you will use it with your children.

3. Plan to lead your group in some type of creative writing. How will you spark their interest? How will you use the finished piece?

*Words in parentheses are those for which pictures may be drawn.

Chapter 6

More Creative Methods

O sing unto the Lord a new song: sing unto the Lord, all the earth.

—Ps. 96:1

Teaching and Learning Through Music

The Bible often speaks of music, both instrumental and singing. It tells how the morning stars sang together when the foundations of the earth were laid (Job 38:4, 7). It contains songs that David, the shepherd boy, sang as he made melody unto the Lord with his voice and harp. It tells how shepherds on the starlit hills of Judea heard the joyous song of the angels, "Glory to God in the highest, and on earth peace, good will toward men."

The Bible tells of songs that brought comfort and cheer in times of trouble. Just before Jesus and His disciples went out into the darkness following the Last Supper, they sang a hymn. When Paul and Silas lay in prison at midnight, with bleeding backs and aching bodies, they sang songs of faith and victory.

Christians of every age and in every circumstance have found courage and consolation through music. Songs of faith have gone around the world bringing the gospel message to people everywhere. Those of every land, tribe, and tongue will one day meet around the eternal throne, there to join in the Alleluia chorus of blessing, honor, glory, and power, to Him who is worthy, and who has put the song of joy in our hearts.

Think of your own experience. How has music helped you in your Christian life? Perhaps it was a song that first

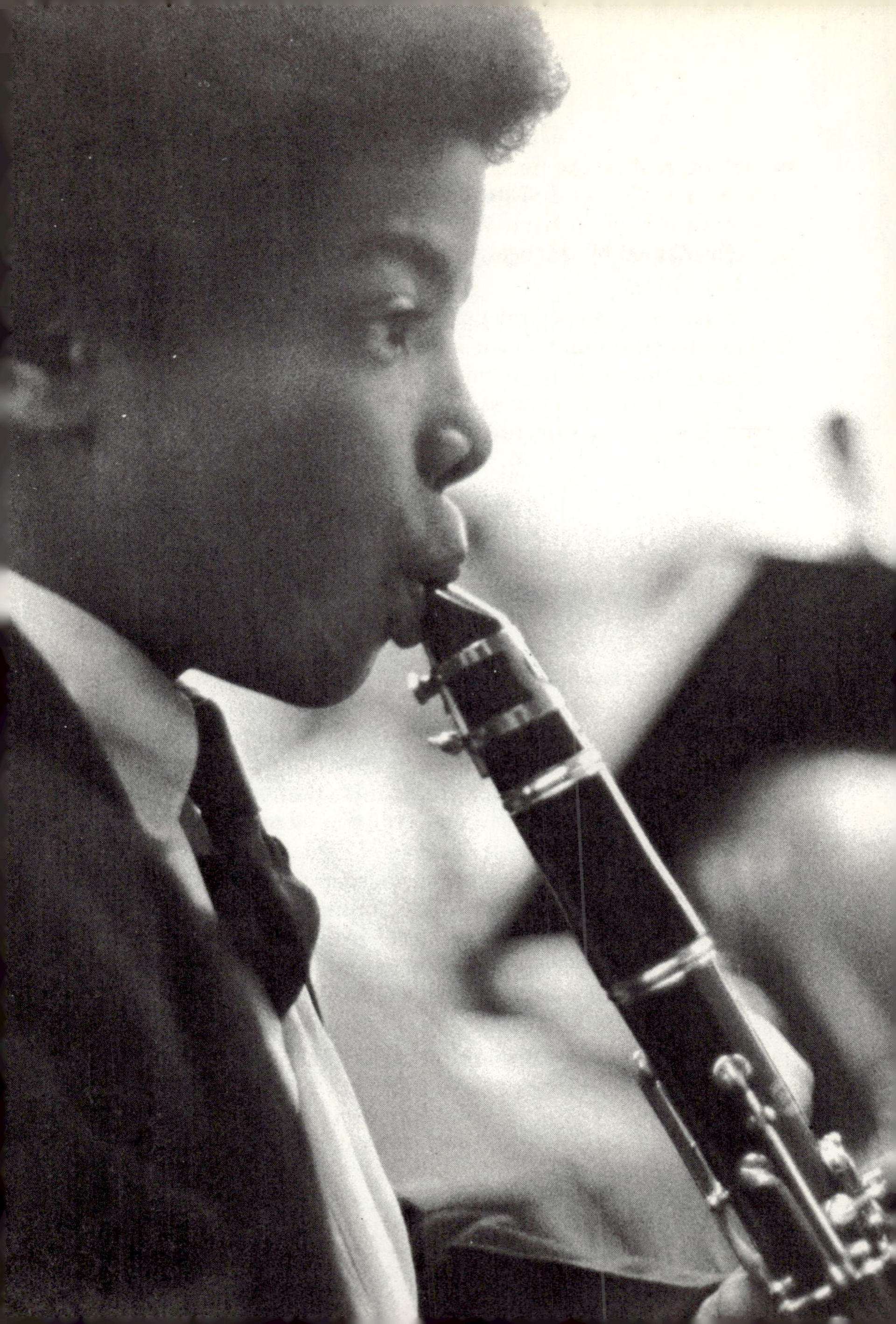

made you realize the need of a Saviour. It may be that a song such as "Take My Life, and Let It Be" brought you to full commitment to Him. Who has not been sustained in an hour of need by the beautiful hymn "O Love That Wilt Not Let Me Go"?

Music is a most vital part of our Christian heritage. It is always important in the spiritual growth of a church. A singing church is a growing church. As a language of worship, it helps us express love, joy, praise, and thanksgiving. It stirs to action and helps us feel secure and triumphant in the love of God. Because it is such an effective medium of expression, we want to share it effectively with our children.

Music gives meaning and value to every experience children have at church. It helps teachers and pupils to develop a fellowship that discovers, enjoys, and worships together. A good music program should be woven into every part of the church's ministry to children.

What Music Does

Music helps children learn more about God, Jesus, the Bible, and our Christian faith. More than any other medium, perhaps, it helps to teach doctrinal truths, clarify concepts, and give spiritual insights and meanings. It helps to establish values and standards of conduct, and ways of living together in happy, friendly ways. Bible verses set to music help children learn and appreciate their meaning. Songs help to interpret and give meaning to units of study.

Music is essential to worship. It helps first of all to create an atmosphere for worship. Songs help children to express their love and praise to God. The right song often helps boys and girls to come to moments of decision and commitment. Songs written especially for children are preferred. Some of the best include "Father, We Thank Thee," "Tell Me the Stories of Jesus," "Jesus, Our Friend," and "God Is Near."

Some of the great hymns of the Church should also be learned and used during primary years. These may include "For the Beauty of the Earth," "Fairest Lord Jesus," "Holy, Holy, Holy," and "There Is a Green Hill Far Away." Still others may be used when there is time for study and explanation. Some of the gospel songs and choruses used in the adult services may also be used, provided they have meaning for the children.

On Sunday Morning

What music experiences may a child enjoy on Sunday morning? As he enters the primary room, soft music may be coming from the record player. He goes to the music center, where he finds an autoharp, melody bells, and other rhythm instruments. A song chart is on an easel nearby. If it is a new song, there may be pictures to help clarify the meaning of thoughts or ideas.

A teacher is at hand to help the child learn to play simple chords on the autoharp to accompany a song that will be used later during worship. Or a teacher may gather some of the children around the piano and go over the words and music to a new song. If the teacher does not sing well, a tape recorder or record player may be used. For the tape recorder, have someone sing the song with a simple piano accompaniment. Play this for the children. Let them listen first and then sing along with the recorder.

In the come-together time, further opportunity is given to learn a new song. The children may choose pictures to illustrate thoughts or phrases; these will be held up before the group at the right time. There may be further discussion of meanings and clarification of ideas. Tone-matching games such as suggested in lesson materials from time to time may be used. If the song calls for action, the children may be guided in suggesting suitable motions. In activity time, they may make scrapbooks to illustrate a song. A frieze may also be made to show a succession of ideas in a song or to illustrate each stanza.

Songs to Use

A good song begins with good words within the understanding of the children. Symbolism should not be used except in rare instances, and then the symbols should be carefully explained. We should avoid words that talk down to children: words such as "little children," and "What do the little birdies say?" The words in children's songs should have strong appeal to the senses. The music should be simple and go well with the words. The range should be between middle C and D in the octave above.

The songs selected for use with the curriculum materials have all been chosen with the best standards in mind. If a teacher uses songs other than those, she should give careful study first to the words and then to the music. Do the words convey proper concepts? Will they help the child to grow in his relationship to God and in Christian living? Is the music good and suited to the words?

Children also enjoy writing simple words and then making up tunes to create their own songs. Sometimes a child makes up a little song at home and brings it to share with the group.

Listening to Music

When worship time comes, the children are often brought into the right mood and feeling by appropriate listening music. This again may be by a record, or by the pianist playing softly. These listening periods are particularly valuable for the child who does not respond readily to other music experiences.

Listening periods deserve more attention than they are usually given. It is a type of experience that may go on through a lifetime, sharpening awareness and creating sensitivity. It opens up an awareness to the "music of the spheres," the song of the meadowlark in the countryside, the snowy tree cricket in the evening hours, the sound of running water, the voices of loved ones.

Creative listening is a blending of enjoyment and appreciation. The listener is involved in an emotional and educational response. It begins with wonder and ends in appreciation.

A teacher sat beside Linda, who was somewhat slow and seldom participated even in the singing experiences. A recording was played with a song about Jesus, beautifully sung. The teacher observed what seemed to be a little quiver of excitement pass through Linda. She looked up at the teacher and said, "Oh, I like that song; don't you?"

Music Meets Special Needs

Music helps the disturbed child to be released from emotional tensions and to open up to healing and growth.

Marcia is a retarded child. Although she seemed to enjoy Sunday school, she was unable or unwilling to enter into any of the activities of the group. She enjoyed music but would not sing or participate in any way. Then one day a miracle happened. Marcia timidly reached out and took a set of wrist bells when it was offered to her. To the delight of everyone, she participated with the group, using the bells to accompany "A Song of Joy." Later she accepted other rhythm instruments.

All the while Marcia was showing marked improvement in her relationships with the teachers and the children. The next big step was responding to a tone-matching game enjoyed by the group. Although she never sang alone, she would stand beside the teacher while the other children sang her part. Eventually Marcia with help could play a few chords on the autoharp. Her parents learned of her progress and bought an autoharp for Marcia to use at home. "How Marcia loves music!" her mother said. "And she sings at home all the time."

Creative Teaching Through Art

Flat Pictures

There is great value in the use of teaching pictures, those supplied through the curriculum materials and those collected by the teacher from other sources. The creative teacher thinks up ways to use these pictures. Much learning occurs through picture study when teacher and children look at a picture together. Sometimes it is wise for the teacher not to say too much too soon, but to let what the child sees speak to him. Even so, a child may need help at first to respond to a picture.

The teacher may need to lead a child from a detached looking to an experience that has real meaning for him. This may be done with well-placed questions. "Did you ever go out of doors at night and look up at the stars? How did you feel? Did God seem near to you? Do you think this is a lonely picture? What makes it seem lonely?" Questions that arouse the senses help a child to grow emotionally as well as intellectually.

Pictures of Bible people and places help children understand customs and ways of living in Bible times. Such pictures help the child to feel at home with Bible people and give a sense of reality to Bible stories.

Pictures are valuable also in helping to teach a new

song. Children may choose appropriate pictures for each stanza or idea in the song.

In research, and in teaching attitudes and standards of behavior, pictures are valuable. Children will refer to them for help in posing their own pictures, or planning simple dramatizations of Bible stories.

As you use flat pictures in your teaching, remember these guidelines: Do not put up too many at one time, and do not leave them up too long. Always be alert for useful pictures wherever you may find them. Also authentic objects to use along with them enhance the value of the pictures. Real objects from the out-of-doors, old coins, antique Bibles, objects from the Holy Land and other faraway places enrich the use of pictures.

Pictures help a child feel a part of the group. A shy child may be brought into the group discussion and activities through the use of right pictures.

Pictures are used for many purposes besides simply looking at them. They may be used in making charts, posters, scrapbooks, friezes, and murals. They may be used to illustrate poems, original stories, or to post on bulletin boards.

Pictures should be mounted to enhance beauty and add durability. The mounting should be simple and not detract from the beauty or interest of the picture itself.

Projected Pictures

Projected pictures are also valuable and should be a part of primary teaching-learning experiences. They should be used wisely and not just to fill in time. Available filmstrips and slide sets are suggested in the lesson materials from time to time. Some are included in *Primary Teaching Resources*.

A teacher should preview all filmstrips and slides

before using them with the children. This enables him to be familiar with the content and to be prepared to guide the children in discussion and evaluation. It is also important to prepare the children for what they will see by listing some things to look for.

An interesting activity is to provide a camera and let the children take their own slides. This could be part of a field trip to help the children record their findings, or could be used to record the dramatization of a story. Simple narration may be written by the children and read as a script with the finished slides. Such scripts may also be recorded on tape by a child, or by a group of children.

Pictures Children Make

When a child has had an emotional experience and new insights have been caught, he wants to express his thoughts and feelings. Creative expression through drawing is an effective means and is usually easily arranged.

The child who is withdrawn or who has other emotional problems sometimes finds release and help through drawing pictures. Also a child's art is often the key to his inner feelings. A child with a poor self-image refused to draw a picture of herself. Another child in the middle of a large family who felt insecure drew a picture of a house without a roof, and trees without roots. These were clues to the teacher that the children had special needs.

Drawings or paintings reflect life as children see it. They reflect feelings, moods, and thoughts. A drawing or painting may also reveal whether a child is forming right or wrong concepts.

Primary children usually draw or paint boldly. They draw the size of characters in proportion to their importance to them.

A good way to help children get started drawing is by

having them do "surprise" pictures. The teacher gives each child something to start with: a leaf, a piece of yarn, a bright piece of paper, a bud from a tree or shrub. The child makes his own picture, using the object in some way, and later shares his "surprise" with the group. This activity is particularly good in connection with a creation unit, or seasonal activities in fall or spring. When the picture is complete, the child may want to write a few words to describe his picture.

A turnover picture chart is an interesting way to recall a unit of study. The children may each draw a picture of one character or incident studied during the unit. These should be drawn on large sheets of paper (18" x 24"), using white or colored newsprint. After the pictures are drawn, they may be clipped to an easel backboard or large piece of plyboard. Or the pictures may be mounted on heavy paper with holes punched about three inches apart on top or side. They can then be held together with loose ring binders or cord.

Another method is to use a two- or three-ring binder cover. Turn the cover inside out and use it as a holder for your pictures, as illustrated. The pages can be larger than the cover. Punch holes in the pages the same distance apart as the rings in the cover. As the pictures are turned, the child tells about his picture. Or the children may work out a script to be read as the pictures are turned. Such pictures may also be made into a large scrapbook. Children should have liberty to express their own ideas. Basic rules for the teacher are: Don't strive for perfection, and don't over-analyze a child's art. The teacher should give help in technique or use of materials only when it helps a child to express what he wants to convey. Remember that motivation is very important; it is basic to a child's urge to create.

Other Art Experiences

Art activities such as finger painting, spatter painting, sponge and string painting are suggested in the lesson materials from time to time. Directions and materials are also given in *Primary Teaching Resources* for making dioramas, peep boxes, mobiles, murals, and friezes. Every teacher should have good books on arts and crafts and refer to them for additional ideas and help. See a list of such books in the bibliography.

Creative Dramatics

Activity for its own sake is never justified in a Sunday school class, where every moment is precious. But activity as a means to a worthy end or goal is always in order.

When creative dramatics is used in this way, it becomes an important part of teaching-learning experiences. Dramatization may be an effective tool in helping to develop Christian attitudes and behavior. It helps to sharpen the child's awareness and sensitivity to the needs of others. Purpose is given to research, learning is motivated, and new insights are gained. Opportunity is provided for cooperation and sharing experiences. Through dramatic play the teacher becomes better acquainted with the children and learns more about their individual and corporate needs.

First graders readily enter into informal dramatics. At home they step into the role of mother, father, teacher, doctor, nurse, astronaut, or pilot. "Let's play like . . ." is a natural expression with them. Thus when the teacher says, "Let's play a Bible story," they are ready at once.

Informal dramatics can be a satisfying and unusual way of learning for teacher and pupil alike. Usually children have new and fresh ideas which develop as the planning moves along. The quiet child who has difficulty participating in other forms of group activity will often come alive and give ideas for informal play. The creative teacher who is sympathetic, enthusiastic, and not afraid to venture, may spark the interest and imagination of the children.

A group of second graders had just listened to a Bible story well told. They followed with great interest as the teacher made the story of King Josiah and the lost book come alive. Then the teacher discussed the story with them:

"How do you suppose Josiah felt when he saw the Temple in ruins?

"Do you suppose the workmen were surprised when Shaphan told them to clean up the Temple?

"How do you think Hilkiah felt when the workmen brought him the Bible scroll?

"Can you imagine how it felt to hold this old, old book in his hands?

"Why did Shaphan take it to the king?

"Why did King Josiah feel sad when he heard the words of the Bible scroll?

"Why did he want all the people to hear the words of the book?

"How did the people feel when they heard the words of the book?

"Would you like to play the story? Who would like to be King Josiah? John would make a good king. Alan, do you want to be king also? We can play the story again later and you may be the king next time. Who would like to be Shaphan? Hilkiah? Some of you may be the workmen. The rest of us can be the people who came together to hear the book read.

"Let's see, do we need anything to help tell the story? A Bible scroll? Yes, we can use the one on the Bible table. What else? A crown for King Josiah? We could make one from some construction paper, couldn't we? Let's see now, King Josiah, you look out the window of your palace and see the old, broken-down Temple. What would you say?"

What steps did this teacher take in preparation for playing the story?

1. The story was well told.
2. The important characters were recalled.
3. Events of the story were highlighted.
4. Suggestions were called for to determine who would play the characters.
5. Simple properties were planned.
6. Children's ideas were praised and implemented.

After playing a story the children may help evaluate the activity. "How did you feel when you were King Josiah? Hilkiah? How did you feel as one of the workmen as you cleaned out the rubbish? How did you feel as one of the people who listened to the reading of the Bible scroll? What does this tell us about our Bible scroll? What does this tell us about our Bible today? Yes, it helps us to be thankful we have a Bible to help us know what is right and wrong. Shall we thank God right now for giving us the Bible?"

Besides the use of Bible stories, present-day stories that teach Christian values and standards are also effective. Missionary stories and stories of other Christian leaders usually have plenty of action and lend themselves well to dramatization.

Pantomime

Pantomime is another effective method of informal dramatics. Children enjoy acting out stories while the teacher or an older primary reads the narration. A tape recorder may be used to record the story and the children may work out appropriate scenes and actions.

A group of first graders enjoyed pantomiming the scenes for the Christmas song "Long, Long Ago." The words were sung softly by the teacher, who also played an accompaniment on the autoharp. The children were first "the olive trees" that swayed softly in the wind outside Bethlehem. The "sheep" lay on the hillside while the shepherds were watching them. The last scene was the manger scene where the Christ child was cradled "long, long ago."

Picture Posing

Picture posing is interesting and a simple way to use informal dramatics. Large teaching pictures are valuable for this activity. The children study a picture, and teachers discuss it with them. "What do you see in this picture? What has happened here? What do you think will happen next? What Bible verse might help these children know the right things to do?"

Then the children may decide on characters and pose the picture by imitating expressions and postures of various persons.

Role Playing

Role playing is an informal type of dramatics particularly suited to helping the child think through problems and situations. The teacher should first establish the situation to be played and the characters to be used. The children act out their parts as they see the roles they are playing. As the children play the different parts, role play offers a good way to discuss feelings and relationships. Problems may be introduced and solutions suggested. Values may be formed as children act out their feelings and solve problems.

Conversation and action should be as simple as possible. The important part is to help children feel as others feel, and to solve their problems in the light of Christian truth.

Research

Research is a means by which teacher and pupil together may go on a quest for information and deeper understanding. This is particularly true for middlers and juniors, but simple research can also be done by primaries.

"What does the Bible tell us?" should be the invitation which leads a primary teacher and pupils to open the Word of God. If the child is to grow and develop in mind, spirit, and body, there must be constant challenge. There must be thinking, studying, and evaluating.

The pupil books afford opportunity for study and research. This may include study in the Bible, Bible dictionary, and concordance. It may involve looking into customs and ways of living in Bible times. It may require a look into history to discover how our Bible came to us. Thought questions are given which will lead the pupil to reflect and give answers.

Children are familiar with such study and thinking in public schools and will respond in Sunday school if opportunity is given.

Research may also involve the bringing in of resource persons to speak to the children and discuss the subject under investigation. During a missionary unit a real missionary becomes a valuable part of the teaching-learning process. A doctor or nurse may be invited when the unit is concerned with stewardship of the body. Public school teachers or librarians can be helpful resource people, and are usually readily available. Persons who have been to the Holy Land have much firsthand knowledge to share with children.

Games

The use of games as a learning procedure is becoming more popular both in secular schools and in Christian education. It is a highly successful method and one by which children learn readily. Such games are not used merely to entertain but to communicate facts, to change attitudes, and to develop skills.

Games may be used to introduce a unit of study and create interest. They may be used during the unit or at the close to review what has been learned. They are effective in helping children to learn or to recall Bible memory verses. Games may help to clarify concepts and reveal what the children are thinking and feeling.

Games often set a mood for learning by relieving tensions and helping the children to work together as a group. Sometimes they can help the child who does not feel at ease to be drawn into the activities.

Games may also be used effectively by bus workers when new children are brought into the Sunday school. Bus ministries should be carefully planned and workers trained so that large busloads of children are not unloaded on the Sunday school without adequate direction and materials. This need not happen if there are sufficient trained workers and plans carefully made in advance. In case of early arrival, bus children may be kept on the bus and engaged in Bible learning games. This is an effective way to help boys and girls who have had little or no Christian home training to become acquainted with Bible people and stories.

There are many types of games recommended in curriculum materials. Bible verse games are suggested where the verses are divided and children are asked to match them. Matching games are also used to fit places and persons with events.

The primary workbooks provide fill-in-the-blanks puzzles, true-or-false statements, finish-the-sentences exercises; and simple crossword puzzles. Riddle games ("Who Am I?" or "Who Said It?") are interesting, especially when used in the larger group. For an alphabet game, print letters of the alphabet on cards. Let each child take a card and say a Bible verse, or tell about a Bible character beginning with that letter.

Well-known games such as ticktacktoe and concentration may be adapted to learning Bible facts and concepts. For ticktacktoe, prepare a board 18" x 18" and divide into the usual nine squares. Prepare separate smaller squares of construction paper or felt with an *X* or an *O* on the front and a question on the back. The children may be divided into groups. They may work together to arrive at their answer, or choose one of the group to answer. They get to place the *X* or *O* in the diagram if they can answer the question correctly.

Games of other lands are useful in a missionary unit to help boys and girls identify with people far away.

Choral Reading

Choral reading with young children may be done quite simply. Divide the children into two groups with perhaps a solo or two. Poems as well as Bible passages may be used in this way.

Choral reading is more meaningful when it follows a special study of a psalm or passage. The children in one primary group were studying a unit on David. They had read about shepherds and shepherd life in Bible times. They had looked at pictures and had played matching games of "then" and "now." They had viewed the filmstrip *Shepherd Life in Bible Times,* and had made a chart of what a good shepherd does for his sheep. Several translations of the twenty-third psalm had been read.

Now they were ready when the psalm was introduced as a memory passage. The chart was reviewed. The teacher then recalled some of the findings which clarified meanings of such verses as "I shall not want" and "He maketh me to lie down in green pastures." The children thought of how a shepherd led his sheep to green pastures for feeding and to cool waters for drinking. When danger was near, the good shepherd protected his sheep.

"This psalm tells us what God is like," said the teacher. "He is like a good shepherd. He loves and cares for us each day. Surely goodness and mercy (lovingkindness) will be with us all the days of our lives."

The memory chart had been prepared with verses 1, 5, and 8 designated as solos. The other verses were assigned alternately to Groups 1 and 2, with the final verse to be given by the entire group.

The choral reading was then used during worship for several sessions. There was no drilling or pressure to memorize. The children gained a clear understanding of the meaning of the psalm and it became a part of their storehouse of Bible selections.

Conversation and Discussion

Conversation with primary children can be most creative and valuable. The teacher who is ready to listen will learn many things about and from the children. Children who come early on Sunday morning often look forward to these times to talk things over with an understanding teacher. Sometimes a child's fears and uncertainties are brought out into the open and a teacher can share his own faith and trust in God. Teachers may also share the joys and excitement of good things that happen at home and at school. Such times build up firm relationships between child and teacher. Values are formed that will remain with a child throughout a lifetime.

Before a session, a teacher needs to read through the lesson materials carefully. Sometimes questions are given; sometimes the teachers need to formulate questions that relate to their own particular group. Then ask guidance from the Holy Spirit to help the children gain new insights and growth in spiritual understanding through discussion.

Discussion that comes from asking the right questions helps children to think. Factual questions such as "What?" "Where?" and "When?" are often necessary to lay the foundation for the important "Why?" questions. Teachers need to be prepared to answer some very profound questions about death, change, tragedies, heaven, and eternal life which the children will very likely ask. The teacher will often need to draw deeply on his own spiritual resources to give right answers. Sometimes it will be necessary to say, "I don't know. God's ways are greater than our ways and we can trust Him."

In asking questions, the teacher accepts any sincere answer from a child even though it may not be the right one. There is never sarcasm, amusement, or putting down of the child. In the best form of discussion, the teacher becomes a moderator and listens in as the children talk with one another in search of answers. This helps a teacher to observe and evaluate attitudes, feelings, and understandings.

One little boy from a broken home asked another from a like situation, "Are you afraid when your mother goes out at night on a date and you are left home with just your little brother?"

"Yes," said the other, "but then I pray and I'm not so scared."

This conversation overheard by the sympathetic teacher gave her new insights into some of the problems of the child of today.

Memorization

How important is memorization of Bible verses and longer passages in Christian teaching today? Is this the best use of our time that we have with the boys and girls? If so, how many verses should a primary child be expected to memorize during a unit, a quarter, a year?

Memorization in Sunday school is not stressed as it was in former years. However, those of us who recall choice Bible verses or promises learned in childhood to help us when we need inspiration and comfort feel that memorization is still important.

The primary curriculum materials list a Bible verse to remember each Sunday. It is not realistic to assume that every child will memorize a verse each week, nor could memory drill to achieve this goal be considered the best use of the time. A teacher should study a unit and select those verses or passages for memorization that are the most meaningful for the children. Plans should then be made to add them to the pupil's storehouse of Bible verses.

One difficulty in memorization today is the many different translations of the Bible in use. A teacher may find several different versions among the Bibles brought by the children on any given Sunday morning. It is well to point out to the children that these versions say the same thing, only somewhat different words are used to express the truth. The King James Version or the *New American Standard Bible* are the most frequently memorized. Any typed verses or charts for the children to memorize should be from one of these two versions, or from another version recommended by the pastor and church board for standard use in the local church.

Bible verses or passages should be explored and thoroughly explained before memorization is attempted.

Pictures may be used to clarify meanings of words or phrases. Games may be introduced to help with memorization or recall. These may include scrambled verses, match-the-endings, fill-in-blanks, and put-together puzzles. Children may draw their own pictures to illustrate meanings and colorful words. Flash cards, and word strips with pictures, help children to memorize. Simple dramatization may also be used to clarify meanings and thus help memorization.

Key verses and longer passages recommended for memorization are usually given in *Primary Activities* take-home sheets. Otherwise the teacher may type up verses and passages for the children to take home to memorize.

Simple rewards may be given occasionally for memorization but these should be kept at a minimum. First of all, the teacher must keep in mind the sensitive, conscientious child who will feel under pressure to memorize everything that is suggested—and is troubled if he can't do it. There is also the child who finds memorization difficult; how can he be made to feel a worthy part of the group if he can't measure up to the accomplishments of the others? And what about the child who through no fault of his own is irregular in attendance? Or the child who has no help or encouragement at home? Such a child must surely feel left out and discriminated against when he is never able to earn an award. The Sunday school teacher should always consider these factors prayerfully when giving rewards for memorization—or any other achievement, for that matter.

A memorization list of Bible verses and longer passages for children, nursery through junior age, has been prepared in pamphlet form. This may be used in Sunday school and other boys' and girls' groups in the church to help children memorize important Bible selections. Order from your denominational department of education.

For Further Study

1. List the songs you use that have Bible verses set to music.

2. Make a list of the songs you will use with your children next Sunday and tell why you have chosen them.

3. Plan to use a new song with your group and tell how you will introduce it.

4. Think of the pictures you plan to use with your present unit of study. How will you use these most effectively? Choose one picture and tell what questions you could use with the children to stimulate thinking.

5. How do you feel about the use of dramatics in your teaching? Explain.

6. Make a list of resource persons in your church or community who could be interviewed or invited to speak to your group.

7. Plan a game to be used as a review of Bible facts, or to change an attitude you have observed in your group.

Bibliography

Allstrom, Elizabeth. *You Can Teach Creatively.* Nashville: Abingdon Press, 1970.

Bolton, Barbara J. *Ways to Help Them Learn.* Glendale, Calif.: G/L Publications, 1972.

Bolton, Barbara J., and Smith, Charles T. *Bible Learning Activities.* Glendale, Calif.: G/L Publications, 1973.

Chamberlain, Eugene. *When Can a Child Believe?* Nashville: Broadman Press, 1973.

Cully, Iris V. *Ways to Teach Children.* Philadelphia: Fortress Press, 1965.

Fulbright, Robert G. *New Dimensions in Teaching Children.* Nashville: Broadman Press, 1971.

Hall, Arlene S. *Toward Effective Teaching—Elementary Children.* St. Louis: Christian Board of Publications, 1969.

Jones, Mary Alice. *The Christian Faith Speaks to Children.* Nashville: Abingdon Press, 1965.

Keiser, Armilda. *Here's How and When.* New York: Friendship Press, 1952.

McDaniel, Elsiebeth. *You and Children.* Chicago: Moody Press, 1973.

Rives, Elsie, and Sharp, Margaret. *Guiding Children.* Nashville: Convention Press, 1969.

Shields, Elizabeth McE. *Music in the Religious Growth of Children.* Nashville: Abingdon Press, 1943.

Stith, Marjorie. *Understanding Children.* Nashville: Convention Press, 1969.

Tobey, Kathrene M. *Learning and Teaching Through the Senses.* Philadelphia: Westminster Press, 1970.